An Immigrant's Guide to

Tax in USA

What you really need to know...

Richard Rubin, Esq.

Any questions or comments can be sent to info@rubinlaw.us

In this book the IRS is frequently portrayed as a Roman Centurion. This metaphor is absolutely tongue-in-cheek.

Over the years I have worked with a large number of people at the IRS, most of whom are a pleasure to work with. Their job is to administer US tax law and procedure, which is a thankless task, due to the complexities and sometimes excesses of the US tax system.

In reality, the Centurion metaphor applies to the rules of the US tax system – which can be very harsh in their application, especially to new entrants.

This book is dedicated to the clients I have worked with on their transition to US taxpayer status. Without them, this book would not have been possible.

I want to thank my colleague and life partner Karin, for her unending patience and support with this book, with the practice, and with me.

I want to thank Barry Adams, for his thoughtful and thorough review of the book; and for the excellent points that he raised in his review.

I want to thank Steph Pai for capturing the message so well, with her wonderfully refreshing and creative sketches.

And last but not least, I want to thank Craig Moonshower, for his painstaking guidance and diligence in designing the book.

Assumptions are what we don't know we are making.

Douglas Adams

PREFACE

When I moved to the United States many years ago, I thought that I was reasonably well prepared for my transition to US tax.

I was wrong.

Although I had spent many years in tax with a large US-based public accounting firm, and had visited the US many times, I was totally unprepared for what I would personally be facing.

Like most other immigrants, I had to learn about US tax as a new entrant through the trials and tribulations of my own personal experience. My ensuing encounters with US tax were unpleasant and costly.

Some years later, when practicing as an attorney, I became aware that clients who were immigrating to the US frequently experienced the same difficulties that I had bumped into years before. I began offering assistance with these issues, and have since worked with a large number of new entrants, who are in the process of acquiring green cards, or moving to the United States. In virtually every case, these people were well on their way to encountering the same difficulties with US tax that I had encountered years before.

This book is aimed at helping you avoid these difficulties – and their costly consequences.

Reading this book will provide you good insight into the issues that you will face on your transition to US taxpayer status. You will, however, need professional assistance.

No responsible person would contemplate undertaking a surgical procedure themselves based on what they have learned from reading a book. In similar vein, you should not attempt your transition to US taxpayer status without obtaining professional assistance.

Richard Rubin

Atlanta, 2019

INTRODUCTION

Most newcomers expect that tax in the U.S. will somewhat resemble the tax system of their home country.

Although the expectation is fairly widespread, it's stronger where the newcomer hails from a country that has significant cultural or language ties with the U.S.

As comforting as the expectation may be, I'm afraid it is largely an illusion; because tax in the U.S. is fundamentally different from tax anywhere else in the world.

In the chapters that follow, you will probably find many aspects of US tax are not what you are expecting, and perhaps not what you were hoping for.

But the earlier you know about these differences, the better. And the fact that you are reading about them, rather than going through hardship from experiencing them (as happens with most new entrants), means that you are way ahead in the queue.

By reading this book, you should be able to avoid many of the harsh tax results that befall new entrants to the United States.

CONTENTS

CHAPTER 3

The Clock is Ticking!

What causes you to become a US taxpayer

CHAPTER 4

Your Makeover – to a US Taxpayer!

Consequences of you becoming a US taxpayer

CHAPTER 7

Foreign Bank Accounts & FBARs

You need to disclose your foreign accounts

CHAPTER 8

Foreign Company Complications

Complications from holding shares in a foreign company

CHAPTER 9

Mutual Fund Mayhem

Punishing treatment for holding foreign mutual funds

CHAPTER 10

Foreign Trust Travails

Harsh US tax treatment of your foreign trust interests

CHAPTER 11

Getting your Ducks in a Row!

Positioning yourself to become a US taxpayer

Appendix, Tax Treaties

AS FAR AS *I'M* AWARE, THESE ARE THE ISSUES...
AND AS FAR AS *I'M* AWARE, *THESE* ARE THE ISSUES...

Chapter 1

In a Nutshell

Key tax issues when moving to the US

By the time most new entrants get to deal with US tax, they have relied upon false assumptions, so they land up having to pay unnecessary amounts of tax, and in many cases, significant penalties as well.

Newcomers who get caught in this way typically include those who are financially savvy, and those with tax experience in other countries.

This is because no amount of smarts, and no amount of home country experience, can prepare new entrants for some unusual aspects of US tax.

To prevent this from happening to you, you need a fundamental understanding of the way US tax and reporting works, especially in relation to your foreign (non-US) assets and structures.

Key is knowing when you will become a US taxpayer

It's fundamentally important that you determine the approximate date upon which you will become a US taxpayer. See *The Clock is Ticking!*

This is important for a variety of reasons, namely:

- The changes in the way that you will be taxed, from that date on;
- The disclosures that you will need to make;
- You may need to sell certain assets or re-arrange certain structures before that date;
- You may be able to defer the date you become a US taxpayer;
- You may already be a US taxpayer, and if so, you may need to come into compliance.

You may already be a US taxpayer without realizing it

Individuals may be seen as US taxpayers, even though they live outside the United States. This usually occurs where the person has a green card.

Where this happens, the new entrants typically arrive in the US to learn that they are already out of compliance, because they should have been filing US returns, and that they may be subject to penalties. See *OOPs! We're Out of Compliance!*

Once you become a US taxpayer, you will be subject to US tax on your worldwide income

As a US taxpayer, you will be subject to US tax in principle on your income from anywhere in the world, including income that you earn – or are regarded as earning – from outside the United States.

- For work and services income, this includes salary, wages and fees, even if the services are performed, and the income is paid, outside the United States.
- For investment income, this includes dividends, interest, royalties and gains, even if the investment is located, and the income is paid, outside the United States.

Your worldwide income will be determined under US rules

You may be subject to tax on income that was earned by a non-US entity, rather than earned by you personally.

This occurs where the income of the non-US entity is imputed to you, or where the entity is classified as a "pass-through". This frequently occurs where:

- The non-US entity is a self-funded trust; or
- You are a partner in a non-US partnership; or
- You own shares in a non-US company that mostly earns royalties or mostly earns dividends, interest, or gains, from portfolio investment. See *Foreign Company Complications.*

Your foreign income <u>and assets</u> are on the table

One of the big surprises in store for new US taxpayers is that they are required to disclose not only their worldwide income, but their worldwide financial assets as well.

I often tell clients that once they become US taxpayers, not only are they reclassified for US tax purposes, but their financial interests are reclassified as well.

The fact that your financial interests may be outside the US, and may have nothing to do with the US, does not excuse them from this reclassification and the disclosure that you will be required to make. In fact, your foreign (non-US) bank accounts and financial assets are subject to far greater disclosure than if you were to have comparable interests in the US. See *Foreign Bank Accounts & FBARs.*

Your bank or institution may have reported your accounts to the IRS

These days, banks / institutions in a number of countries routinely report their clients' accounts to the IRS, as required under FATCA agreements that have been concluded with these countries. FATCA is a cross-border reporting mechanism between the US and a large number of countries. It's clear that FATCA reporting has been quite effective, at least by some countries. See *FATCA is No Fantasy.*

If you have accounts in a country that has subscribed to FATCA, your accounts may already have been reported to the IRS – if your bank or institution has reason to believe that you are becoming a US taxpayer, or that you are moving to the United States.

Where this happens, the IRS will have your foreign account data against which your disclosures may be compared.

As a practical matter, the chances of such a comparison taking place increase dramatically where your bank / institution has, or will obtain, your social security number.

Some foreign investments are just not suited to the US

The harsh reality is that some non-US investments are simply not suited to the US tax system.

All too often, this problem only becomes apparent when new entrants are having their first tax returns prepared. But by then it's typically too late, and it's usually a matter of facing the consequences.

The key is timing. You need to be aware of this issue early in the process, preferably before you become a US taxpayer. This will allow you to divest yourself of these assets before you become a US taxpayer, rather than be caught as a victim of the harsh US tax treatment simply because you own such investments.

Although there are a number of foreign assets that can cause you a US tax headache, at the top of the list are foreign mutual funds. Depending upon the country and market segment, these investments may be known as mutual funds, hedge funds, unit trusts, or simply funds. See *Mutual Fund Mayhem*.

Some foreign structures are not suited to the US

In similar vein, some non-US structures are simply not well suited to the US tax system.

As with unsuited investments, usually this problem comes to light when newcomers are having their first tax returns prepared. And by then it's typically too late, so it's usually a matter of facing the consequences.

Although there are a number of foreign structures that have negative US tax consequences, at the top of the list are non-US trusts. Depending upon the country formed and their function, these entities may be locally known under a variety of names, including foundations, treuehands, funds, and family trusts. See *Foreign Trust Travails.*

Again, the key is timing. You need to be aware of this issue before you become a US taxpayer. In many cases, this will allow you to restructure before you become a US taxpayer, and so avoid the usual harsh US tax consequences.

Beware claiming Tax Treaty benefits to reduce your US tax

Many new entrants to the United States hail from countries that have a Tax Treaty with the United States. And most Tax Treaties allow for a reduction in US tax under certain circumstances.

If you come from a Treaty country, you may well be tempted to claim a reduction in US tax under the Treaty.

But if you have or will acquire a green card, claiming Treaty relief is not for you. Even if you qualify in every respect for relief under a Treaty with your home country, claiming this relief is likely to jeopardize your green card. See *Your Makeover – to a US Taxpayer!*

US tax and disclosure rules are not Intuitive

It is not generally a good idea to rely on rationalizations about US tax consequences or disclosures.

US tax law and regulations sprawl across 80,000 pages or so, about 30 or 40 times the size of the tax systems in most other countries.

As a result, most structures and transactions that impact US taxpayers tend to be impacted by a large number of statutory provisions.

The resultant tax treatment and disclosure requirements are seldom intuitive. Decisions based on simple rationalizations are unlikely to work well and may bring about unintended consequences.

Tax and filings are taken seriously in the US

In one or two recent cases that have been publicized, individuals in countries abroad have achieved Robin Hood-type celebrity status with risky tax schemes.

This makes for interesting reading.

In the US, tax and filing obligations are taken very seriously, a lot more seriously than in most other countries.

While a cavalier attitude to tax and disclosure may be tolerated in some foreign countries, I don't suggest that you follow this approach in the United States.

APPLICATION
VISA FORM
RECEPTION
U.S.A. IMMIGRATION ATTORNEYS
VISA APPLICATION
I ASSUME U.S. TAX IS FAIRLY SIMPLE!
YES, IT'S PROBABLY SIMILAR TO OUR TAX!

Chapter 2

Assumptions to Avoid

Harmful assumptions – easily made

While US tax rules are unusually tough and far-reaching, the main reason new entrants land up in hot water is because they have relied upon invalid assumptions.

The most harmful assumption anyone can make is that he or she does not make assumptions!

The fact that you may speak good English, are well travelled, and have experience dealing with tax in other countries, will not necessarily save you from falling into one or other of these assumption traps.

Outlined below are some of the more common – yet invalid – tax assumptions that people make when moving to the US.

If any of them ring a bell, it's a good thing you're reading this book!

Invalid Assumption 1

Logically, I don't need to disclose this / this is not taxable

People usually make this assumption in relation to their foreign (non-US) income and assets, especially where the assets were acquired before becoming a US taxpayer.

This assumption is generally invalid because once you become a US taxpayer, your worldwide assets and income are on the table. Not only are *you* reclassified, but your *assets* are as well.

Invalid Assumption 2

US tax must be broadly similar to tax back home

People tend to assume that the tax system that they are entering, will be somewhat similar to the logic of the tax system that they are used to.

Unless the comparison is made philosophically, from 30,000 feet, this assumption will seldom be valid.

US tax and disclosure rules tend to be significantly more complex and detailed than other country rules. In many cases the rules have mutated, so the underlying logic is no longer discernable.

So, at a practical level, US tax rules tend to differ significantly from the rules of other countries. For example, the US tax treatment of non-US resident green card holders, of non-US trusts, and of accruals generally, are only a few of the many differences. See *Your Makeover – To a US Taxpayer!*

Invalid Assumption 3

I have sufficient experience and smarts to deal with US tax myself

Having been with Arthur Andersen for a number of years before moving to the US, I confess to having made this assumption myself. I thought I could handle my transition to US tax.

Fortunately, a friend persuaded me to seek professional assistance, and I'm glad I did so. It was a good decision.

And this was a long time ago, long before the focus on foreign assets and penalties on foreign disclosures, which started with the 2008 indictment of UBS bank and a number of their US account holders, and has since spread to a number of other foreign banks.

Invalid Assumption 4

The IRS will contact me and tell me what I need to do

No they won't.

Any assumption based on the IRS taking proactive steps when you arrive is absolutely false.

It's up to you to ascertain what needs to be done, and to make the required filings with the IRS.

The IRS will give you no leeway if you happen to miss a filing date. The penalty for late filing most of the cross-border disclosure forms is generally $10,000. See *Your First Return*.

Invalid Assumption 5

I'm sure the IRS will understand that I'm new and uninformed

The US tax and disclosure rules that you need to comply with are objective, so it makes no difference whether you are informed or not.

Not knowing about your tax and filing obligations may be of limited assistance, and likely of no assistance, in relation to penalties.

Invalid Assumption 6

Things will sort themselves out

Most tax and disclosure issues don't get better over time, and seldom if ever self-rectify; if anything, they tend to get worse. In some cases, they brew and hatch into issues that are larger and more problematic.

So, if you suspect that you may have a US tax or reporting issue, possibly because you did not take advice, don't assume that the problem will go away. It won't.

You need to be proactive here. A dispute with the IRS carries the potential for penalties and can impact your life in your new country in many ways, including your immigration status.

If you have fallen out of compliance, see *OOPs! We're Out of Compliance!*

Invalid Assumption 7

Why should I disclose this to the IRS? It's none of their business!

Frequently new entrants resist – and may even resent – that they need to disclose to the IRS their income and assets outside the United States.

The US tax and Treasury codes create a legal obligation on US taxpayers to disclose all their income, as well as certain financial assets, even if these are outside the United States.

By becoming a US taxpayer, your foreign income and foreign assets become the IRS' business.

Invalid Assumption 8

No need to disclose my foreign stuff – the IRS will never find out!

While it's true that the US tax system is essentially based on self-reporting, over the last few years the introduction of FATCA, and the expansion of information treaties, has resulted in the IRS having more effective access to foreign account / income information.

Under FATCA, foreign accounts that are owned, or suspected of being owned, by US taxpayers are routinely reported by the foreign entity to the IRS. And when they are reported, the IRS typically cross-checks the details to the taxpayers' returns.

So, once you become a US taxpayer, any decision not to disclose based upon an assumption that the IRS will not find out is simply a bad one.

The question more properly stated is *how* to report your foreign income and financial assets, not *whether* to report them.

Invalid Assumption 9

Good thing I put my assets into a trust before moving to the US. Now I don't have to report the assets or the income!

New entrants sometimes transfer some of their assets into a foreign trust before moving to the US, based on the assumption that the assets, income from the assets, and the transfer will not need to be reported to the IRS.

Unfortunately, that's not what the law says. Where individuals transfer assets to a foreign trust and then become US taxpayers, the tax code deems the transfers to take place after they become US taxpayers.

As a result, people in this category have to report the transfer for the year they become US taxpayers, and also have to report their interest in the foreign trust each year going forward. See *Foreign Trust Travails, Pre-immigration Trusts.*

Invalid Assumption 10

No need to file US tax returns if you don't live in the United States

Sometimes individuals land up being US taxpayers while living outside the United States.

This may happen, for example, where a US citizen lives outside the US, or where an individual has obtained a green card, by lottery or otherwise, and remains living in his home country.

The people to whom this applies frequently assume that they are not required to file US tax returns and Foreign Bank Account Reports (FBARs), because they are not living in the United States.

Nothing could be more wrong. Once you become a US taxpayer, you are expected to file US returns and FBARs, irrespective of where you happen to live.

Invalid Assumption 11

No need to file US returns if you file returns in another country. That would be double tax!

People who file foreign country tax returns frequently assume that by doing so, they need not file US tax returns.

Unfortunately, filing foreign country returns does not satisfy your obligation to file US tax returns and FBARs once you are a US taxpayer.

If you pay tax in a foreign country, this may well reduce your US tax liability on foreign country income, by way of a foreign tax credit. If the foreign tax you paid is more than your US tax, don't assume that it will completely cover your US tax, because the US foreign tax credit rules contain various limitations. See *Your Makeover! To a US Taxpayer!, Foreign Tax Paid.*

But even if you are entitled to a foreign tax credit that fully covers the US tax that you would otherwise owe, you still need to file US returns and claim the credit on your US returns. You will also need to file FBARs.

Invalid Assumption 12

I'm receiving a gift / inheritance from my family abroad. Surely this has nothing to do with the IRS?

People often assume that gifts or inheritances from family who live abroad are a private matter, which has nothing to do with the IRS.

These assumptions are false. Once you are a US taxpayer, you need to report foreign gifts and inheritances that you receive above certain thresholds, even though they are not taxable.

Failing to report them is likely to attract penalties, and occasionally may cause gifts to be regarded as taxable. It may also cause an IRS audit.

Invalid Assumption 13

I'm making a gift to family from my assets abroad. Surely this has nothing to do with the IRS?

Once you are a US taxpayer, you need to report gifts that you make, including foreign gifts, above certain thresholds, even though they are not generally taxable.

Hopefully you have reported the account from which you are making the gift on your tax returns and FBARs.

HOW MANY DAYS HAVE WE SPENT IN THE U.S. OVER THE LAST THREE YEARS?
ARE THESE OUR GREEN CARDS? CAN'T BE! THEY'RE NOT GREEN!
TIK TOK
USCIS
ID
TRAVEL ITINERARY

Chapter 3

The Clock is Ticking!

What causes you to become a US taxpayer

Those who are on the road to becoming US taxpayers typically face a number of concurrent challenges.

Typically, the change to US taxpayer status takes place around the time of arranging for immigration visas or green cards, leaving your home country, and relocating to the US.

But you may become a US taxpayer simply through extended vacations or business visits to the United States, even if you have no intention of becoming US resident.

The rigors of these challenges sometimes result in new entrants overlooking the fact that their tax status is also changing, and what they should be doing about it.

Becoming a US taxpayer

Becoming a US taxpayer means that you are becoming US tax resident.

You will become a US taxpayer if and when you satisfy any of the criteria outlined below under *Factors leading to US taxpayer status*.

Whether you intend to become a US taxpayer is not generally relevant

- As appears below, the factors that bring about US taxpayer status are mostly objective.
- So, whether or not you want to become a US taxpayer, or know that you are becoming a US taxpayer, is generally irrelevant in determining whether you actually become a US taxpayer.

Unwitting US taxpayers

- Because US taxpayer status comes about due to objective factors, people frequently become US taxpayers without wishing or intending their new US tax status.
- These same objective factors sometimes lead to individuals becoming US tax payers without realizing it, and as a result they become "unwitting US taxpayers".
- In part, this is because no-one tells you that you are a US taxpayer, or that are about to become one.

Consequences of being an unwitting US taxpayer

- Where unwitting US taxpayers only get to learn of their US taxpayer status some months or years after the change, they are typically out of compliance with their US filings, and may also be liable for outstanding US tax as well as penalties.
- Furthermore, those who land in this position have also missed out on the opportunity to plan and position themselves for the change in their tax status.

Factors leading to US taxpayer status

If you fall into any of the categories outlined below, by doing so you will have become a US taxpayer:

Acquiring a Green Card

The most common way of becoming a US taxpayer is by acquiring a green card.

- A green card means that you have been recognized as a Permanent Resident with the USCIS (previously the INS) for US immigration purposes.
- It also means that you have been recognized as a US taxpayer with the IRS for US tax purposes.
- Loosely speaking, you will be considered a US taxpayer for most purposes once you have been issued a green card.
- However, strictly speaking, your US taxpayer status commences on the first day that you are physically present in the US after your green card has been issued.

Becoming a US Citizen

- Becoming a US citizen gives rise to US taxpayer status, if you are not already a US taxpayer.
- Individuals born in the US are generally US citizens at birth, and as a result, are typically US taxpayers at birth.
- For those who were not born in the US, US citizenship is generally preceded by acquiring a green card; and acquiring a green card typically creates US taxpayer status. See above.
- However, if you weren't born in the US, but were born to US citizen parents, you may have become a US citizen while living outside the US without acquiring a green card. In these cases, becoming a US citizen will give rise to US taxpayer status.

Living in the US

- You may become a US taxpayer by living or staying in the US, even if you don't have a green card and are not a US citizen.

- Here the test for US taxpayer status is based on a time-related formula, although there are a few rules that sometimes override the formula.

  Time-Related Formula

  - Your stay in the US may cause you to become a US taxpayer, according to the rules of a formula which works as follows:

    - Each day that you were present in the US during the current year, is taken into account as 1 day;

    - Each day that you were present in the US during the year preceding the current year, is taken into account as 1/3 day;

    - Each day that you were present in the US during the year two years before the current year, is taken into account as 1/6 day.

  - Using the above formula, if the total number of days derived exceeds 183, then in principle you have become a US taxpayer based on your physical presence in the US.

  - However, there are exceptions that may override this result. These are outlined below.

  Closer Connection Exception

  - If you can show that you had a "closer connection" to a foreign country for any of the days included in the formula, then those days may be excluded from the calculation.

- To exclude these days, you generally need to make affirmative filings with the IRS, within certain time limits, failing which you may be denied the exclusion.

Student / Teacher / Trainee Exceptions

- If you are a student, teacher or trainee who is in the US on an F visa, J visa, M visa, or Q visa, you may be able to exclude the days you are present in the US on this visa, provided you comply with the terms of the visa.

- The number of years you may be able to exclude from the formula is limited depending upon the circumstances.

Medical Exception

- If you can show that the reason you stayed in the US was due to medical necessity, then the days in question may be excluded from the calculation.

- The condition preventing you from leaving must have arisen while you were in the US.

- To exclude these days, you generally need to make affirmative filings with the IRS, within certain time limits, failing which you may be denied the exclusion.

Foreign Government / International Organization Employee Exceptions

- If you are an employee of a foreign government with diplomatic status, you may be able to exclude from the calculation the days that you were present in the US and were employed as such.

- Similarly, if you are an employee of certain recognized international organizations, you may be able to exclude from the calculation the days that you were present in the US and were employed as such.

Professional Athlete Exception

- Professional athletes who are present in the US to compete in charitable sports events can exclude from the calculation the days that they compete.

Treaty "Exception"

- If you come from a country with which the US has a Tax Treaty, you may be able to claim that the terms of the Treaty apply to prevent you from becoming a US taxpayer. Beware doing so if you hold a green card. See *Your Makeover – To a US Taxpayer!, Green Card Holders*.

Electing to be a US taxpayer

- It occasionally happens that an individual, who is not a US taxpayer under any of the above criteria, actually wishes to become a US taxpayer.

- In the majority of these cases, the person wishing to become a US taxpayer is married to someone who is a US taxpayer, or is becoming a US taxpayer.

- If you are married to a US taxpayer (who already has a green card or is a US citizen), you can become a US taxpayer simply by filing a joint return with your spouse, and making a written election with the return.

- If you are not married to a US taxpayer, you can become a US taxpayer by filing a return and making a written election with the return.

  You need to have spent at least 75% of the days in the United States for the year of election, beginning with (and including) a period of at least 31 consecutive days of presence in the US. Depending upon the circumstances, you may be required to spend additional time in the US during the year following the year of election.

Delaying the date that you become a US taxpayer

- Once you have determined which of the above categories applies to you, depending upon your personal circumstances you may well be able to influence the date on which you become a US taxpayer.

- In most cases, this means taking steps to delay the date that you will become a US taxpayer.

- Your ability to do so may be limited by family, travel, work, financial, and other practical considerations.

- If you are becoming a US taxpayer because you are acquiring a green card, and you are outside the United States when the green card is issued, delaying your US taxpayer status may be achieved simply by remaining outside the US.

  Make sure to consult an immigration attorney to ensure that the period you remain outside the US after your green card has been issued doesn't jeopardize your green card.

- If you are becoming a US taxpayer because you have been living or staying in the United States, delaying your US taxpayer status may be either achieved by departing the US, or by making sure that you qualify for one of the exceptions mentioned above under *Time Related Formula*.

  Be aware that if you intend to rely upon one of these exceptions, you generally need to make an affirmative filing that claims the exception at the time you file your return for that year.

No halfway house

- While you may well be able to influence the date on which you become a US taxpayer, there is no interim or halfway status. When the change in status happens, it happens completely.

- Mention is made of this because people who intend moving to the US sometimes precede their move by investing in the US, for example in US stocks or real estate, or by taking an interest in a US business.

- There's nothing wrong with investing in the US prior to moving. It may be a convenient way to gain experience, a foothold into some aspect of the market, or a means of building an asset base in the US.

- It may also be that investing in the US is a necessary step in the process for you to obtain an E-2 visa or to obtain a green card under the EB-5 program.

- But no matter what your motive for investing in the US may be, the investment will not ease your transition to US taxpayer status.

- By investing in the US prior to your move, you will initially have the tax status of a nonresident investor, which is fundamentally different from the status of a US taxpayer. As a nonresident investor, the tax rules applicable to you and the returns you will have to file are quite different from those that will apply to you once you become a US taxpayer.

NEW ARRIVALS! THIS WAY, PLEASE!
ENTRANCE
TAXPAYERS' MAKEOVER UNIT
OUR MAKEOVERS ARE REALLY LIFECHANGING
WE PROMISE A WHOLE NEW YOU
WITH RECLASSIFIED INVESTMENTS
WE'RE JUST LIKE ALL THE OTHER NEWCOMERS!
YES, BUT LOOK AT HOW *THINGS CHANGE* AFTER THEY BECOME *U.S. TAXPAYERS*

Chapter 4

Your Makeover – to a US Taxpayer!

Consequences of you becoming a US taxpayer

The day you transition to US taxpayer status will be a normal day. The sun will rise in the East in the normal way, and the birds will chirp the way they normally do.

Most people are blissfully unaware - at least at the time that they become US taxpayers - of their change in tax status.

This is hardly surprising, seeing as no-one typically informs you of your change in status – at least not at the time your status changes. Yet the change is fundamental, and permanent.

The most usual way of becoming a US taxpayer is by being issued a green card. Unfortunately, there is absolutely no mention or suggestion on the green card, nor in the letter that accompanies it, that your tax status is changing.

Consequences are far-reaching

- Not only are most people unaware that they have become US taxpayers, they are also generally unaware of the consequences attaching to their change in tax status.

- This can be tough, seeing as the consequences of becoming a US taxpayer are far-reaching and permanent.

- Upon transitioning to a US taxpayer, not only will you be reclassified for US tax purposes, but your assets and financial interests will effectively be "reclassified" as well.

- This includes assets and interests that you acquired from non-US sources before you became a US taxpayer, and other assets and interests that are outside the US.

  The sheer reach of the US tax system can be difficult to accommodate. People ask, for example:

  - What has the IRS to do with the money that I earned in years gone by?

  - Or with the shares that I received on selling my business?

  - Or with the assets that I inherited?

  The simple answer is that the IRS does have potential interest in these assets, which arises through you, once you become a US taxpayer.

- As a result of this "reclassification" of your assets and interests, you may be subject to US tax on income earned by a foreign entity, in which you have an interest, even though you don't actually receive the income.

- Aside from tax returns, you will be required to file a large number of other forms to disclose your interests in foreign bank accounts and foreign financial assets. The IRS takes these forms seriously, and heavy fines are imposed for failing to file the forms, or for unreported foreign financial assets.

Tax on Worldwide Income

Once you become a US taxpayer, you will be taxed in the US on your worldwide income.

This means that all income that you earn, of all types, and from all countries, is typically taxable.

Your worldwide income is determined under US rules. Some of these more significant rules are outlined below.

Tax on Cash Receipts

- Like most other US taxpayers, you will likely pay tax on a "cash receipts" basis.

  With certain exceptions, this means that you will be subject to tax on income that you actually receive, or constructively receive.

  An example of a constructive receipt would be where income is paid to a third party on your behalf.

- Even though you pay tax on a cash receipts basis, if you're a partner in a partnership, you will be taxed on your allocation of partnership net income, irrespective of whether you actually receive it.

  A foreign entity that is not a partnership in the foreign country may be regarded as a partnership in the United States.

- If you expect to receive payment of significant income shortly after you become a US taxpayer, you should generally take steps to receive it before you become a US taxpayer – which may entail delaying the date you become a US taxpayer. See *Getting your Ducks in a Row!, Your US taxpayer status*, and *The Clock is Ticking!, Delaying the date that you become a US taxpayer*.

Income Earned by Foreign Entities

Where income is earned by a foreign entity, in which you are seen to have a significant interest, the income may be imputed to you, with the result you may be subject to tax on this income, even though you have not received it and may never receive it.

- For example, income that is earned by a non-US trust may be taxed to you, even though you never receive it, if you are seen as the Grantor of the trust. See *Foreign Trust Travails*.

- And income that is earned by a non-US company may be taxed to you, even though you never receive it, if the company is seen as controlled by you. See *Foreign Company Complications*.

Tax Rates

The commonly applied tax rates for individuals are as follows:

- Income tax on ordinary income - 10% to 37%, which is reached at income above $500,000 ($370,000 if married filing separately and $600,000 if married filing jointly).

- Income tax on long-term capital gains and dividends – generally 15% or 20%.

- Net Investment Income Tax (NIIT) – 3.8% on investment income above certain thresholds.

- Social security tax on salary – 12.4% for salary up to about $120,000, of which half is paid by the employer;

- Medicare tax on salary – 2.9%, of which half is paid by the employer;

- Self-employment tax on self-employment income – 15.3%;

- State income tax – generally in the region of 3% – 8%, but occasionally higher (depending on the State and levels of income; for example, California goes up to 13%).

  There's no State income tax in Alaska, Florida, Nevada, South Dakota, Texas, Washington and Wyoming.

Foreign Tax Paid

You will generally be allowed a credit against your US (federal) income tax for any foreign (non-US) income tax that you pay:

- This credit is limited to foreign income tax (so foreign sales tax, VAT, property tax, wealth tax, etc do not qualify for the credit).

- The credit is limited to the foreign tax that you are legally liable to pay, and that is non-refundable. So, for example, if foreign tax was withheld on a payment to you, and you can claim a refund of the foreign tax, you cannot claim a credit for the foreign tax – irrespective of whether you claim the refund.

- Foreign tax paid on your active income (salary and fees) can generally be credited against US tax on your active income; but it cannot be credited against US tax on your passive income (income from investments).

- Foreign tax paid on your passive income can generally be credited against US tax on your passive income; but it cannot be credited against your active income.

- Where you have paid foreign tax on your foreign income, you will still have a "residual" US tax liability, if the foreign tax rate is less than the US tax rate on that income, or where one of the other rules limiting foreign tax credits applies.

- Tax paid to a limited number of foreign countries cannot be claimed as a credit. At the time of writing this book, these countries include Iran, Libya, North Korea, Sudan, and Syria.

Deductions

Most business expenses are deductible from your business income. Salary is not regarded as business income.

The following common non-business expenses are also deductible by claiming them as Itemized Deductions:

- medical and dental expenses, but only to the extent they exceed 7.5% of your gross income;

- home mortgage interest on loans up to $750,000 ($375,000 if married filing separately);
- state and local tax up to $10,000;
- charitable contributions made to recognized charitable institutions.

  As an alternative to claiming Itemized Deductions, you may instead claim a Standard Deduction of $12,000 ($24,000 if married filing jointly). Standard Deductions are available irrespective of how much you spent on the above.

Capital Gains

If you make a gain on the sale of a capital asset, the gain is generally subject to tax.

- The tax on capital gains is a flat rate, generally of 15% or 20%, depending upon your level of other income.
- The taxable gain is generally the difference between the cost of the item, and its selling price.
- You are not permitted a "step-up" for any increases in value that may have taken place prior to you becoming a US taxpayer.
- Where you sell your primary residence, the first $500,000 of gain ($1,000,000 if married filing jointly) is exempt from tax.
- If you have assets that have appreciated significantly in value since the time you acquired them, you should consider selling them before you become a US taxpayer. See *Getting your Ducks in a Row!, Your assets that have increased in value.*

Foreign Services

Income you earn from services performed outside the United Sates are subject to US tax after you become a US taxpayer.

- However, if you live outside the United States and earn a foreign salary or self-employment income, you may qualify for the Foreign Earned Income Exclusion (FEIE) of up to $100,000. You may also be able to deduct foreign housing amounts.
- To qualify for a FEIE you need to be a bona fide resident of the foreign country, or you need to spend more than 11 months of the year there. (If you have a green card, satisfying these requirements may place your green card in jeopardy).
- If you decide to claim a FEIE, you cannot claim a Foreign Tax Credit for the foreign tax that you paid on the income subject to the FEIE.

Foreign Retirement Funds

If you expect to receive payment from a foreign pension fund or retirement payment:

- The payment will likely be treated as ordinary income in the US, and subject to ordinary tax rates, even though it may be exempt, or subject to preferential treatment, in your home country. (However, you may qualify for a reduction in US tax under a Treaty – see below)
- As a result, these payments frequently give rise to a significant US tax liability, especially when paid as a lumpsum.
- You may qualify for reduced US tax on your foreign pension fund or retirement fund payment if you come from a country with which the US has a Tax Treaty, and the Treaty provides relief for the type of payment you receive. (But if you hold a green card, you should not claim Treaty relief – see below).

Green Card Holders

If you hold a green card, or are about to acquire one, you need to be aware of the following:

Don't Make Tax Treaty Claims

- You may be entitled to claim relief from US tax under a Tax Treaty between the US and your home country.
- Even though you may be entitled to Treaty relief, you should not generally claim it.
- This is because most Treaty relief relies upon you being seen as tax resident in a foreign country, or on you not being seen as resident in the United States.
- Claiming Treaty relief generally implies that you are not resident in the US, which potentially conflicts with your US Permanent Resident status, and will likely place your green card in jeopardy.
- You should therefore not generally claim Treaty relief without first taking advice. This is not a tax rule, it is aimed at preventing you from jeopardizing your green card.

A young couple moved from England to CT
To take advantage of the favorable Treaty
But with green cards they were damned
So with taxes they were slammed
The call to come home they felt just like ET.

≈

Don't File a Non-resident Return

- Once you become a US taxpayer, you should generally file Form 1040 on an annual basis. Form 1040 is a regular income tax return, to be distinguished from Form 1040NR, which is a non-resident return.

- Once you have a green card, you should not file Form 1040NR for two separate reasons:

    - Firstly, as a US taxpayer you are expected to file Form 1040, so filing Form 1040NR is inappropriate. Filing Form 1040NR will generally mean that you will be seen as not having filed a return, and you may be subject to penalties for not having done so.

    - Secondly, because Form 1040NR is a nonresident return, filing this form may be seen as an assertion that you are nonresident, which is potentially in conflict with your green card, and may place it in jeopardy.

Make Sure You Remain in Tax Compliance

- While all US taxpayers should remain in tax compliance by paying the required tax and filing the required forms, this has particular relevance to green card holders.

- Not complying with your tax and tax filing obligations may place your green card in jeopardy.

Other Federal Taxes

In addition to the frequently encountered taxes discussed under Tax Rates above, there are a number of other taxes that apply under specific conditions.

Of these, the following deserve mention:

- "Throwback Tax". If you receive a distribution from a foreign non-grantor trust, it may be "thrown back" to the years that the trust earned the underlying income. *See Foreign Trust Travails.*

- "Excess Distribution Tax". This is a tax on "excess distributions" you may receive from a foreign mutual fund, and on any gain you may make when the foreign mutual fund investment is sold. See *Mutual Fund Mayhem.*

- Alternative Minimum Tax (AMT). AMT is a system that runs in parallel to income tax, to ensure you pay tax of at least 26% on income above certain thresholds.

State and Local Taxes

Most States and a small number of cities levy income tax on individuals.

- Becoming a US taxpayer does not of itself generally bring about State or Local tax paying responsibilities, nor does it generally bring State or Local return filing responsibilities.

- State and Local responsibilities are generally triggered by residing in that area, or by earning income in that area.

- Definitions of residence vary between States. Depending on the State, you may be regarded as residing there after only a short period of stay, especially if the State looks to other indicators to establish residency.

- Alaska, Florida, Nevada, South Dakota, Texas, Washington and Wyoming don't levy income tax on individuals who simply live there.

MAYBE SEPARATELY... BUT I'M NOT SURE!
FILING HEAD OF HOUSEHOLD
MARRIED FILING SEPARATELY
MAYBE JOINTLY... WHAT DO YOU THINK?
MARRIED FILING JOINTLY
FILING SINGLE

Chapter 5

Your Tax Filing Status

Selecting the category that applies to you

Many people around the world speak English, but not always the same English.

Shortly after I arrived in the United States, I remember someone asking me "What's your filing status?"

My mind raced through the possibilities. I must have looked bemused, because she clarified the question: "What's your ***tax*** *filing status?"*

I again wondered what she was asking. Was I up to date filing tax returns? Had I paid my tax? Was I a tax resident?

I was in the process of learning that tax filing status refers to the category of filer that you select (or may be forced to select) on your tax return.

There are five different types of filing status, and depending upon your circumstances, you may be able to choose between one or two of them.

If You are Married

- One of the first questions likely to arise once you become a US taxpayer is your tax filing status. And central to the question of your tax filing status is your marital status.
- If you are married, you and your spouse can choose that the two of you will file your US tax returns jointly (Married Filing Jointly).
- Alternatively, you and your spouse can choose that each of you will file your own tax returns (Married Filing Separately).

Married Filing Jointly

- The main effect of filing jointly is that your income is combined with that of your spouse. Tax is then levied on the combined amount, but at a rate that is lower than if you had earned the same amount yourself.
- Most married couples choose Married Filing Jointly as their filing status, because the tax they pay by doing so is generally lower than the combined tax on each of their incomes if they filed separately.
- If you or your spouse earns little or no income, combining your incomes will have little or no effect, and you will benefit from the lower Married Filing Jointly rate. Under these circumstances, Married Filing Jointly is very likely the best filing status for you.
- Conversely, where you and your spouse each earn significant income, your combined income will be in a higher tax bracket, which tends to negate the lower Married Filing Jointly rates and may result in you paying more tax than if you file separately. In cases like this, it may be more beneficial for each of you to file separately.
- If you and your spouse both earn significant income, you should get your return preparer to calculate which status is better for you.
- A further though minor advantage of filing jointly is that you and your spouse then have only one federal return (and one State return) to file each year.

- Should you decide to file your taxes jointly, the chances are that you will still have to file your FBARs separately, assuming you and your spouse both have foreign bank accounts. Although spouses can file a joint FBAR, to do so they both have to own all the foreign accounts.

Married Filing Separately

- Aside from cases where tax savings may be achieved because both spouses earn significant income, Married Filing Separately may be appropriate for you for other reasons, outlined below.
- If you are a US taxpayer, but your spouse is not a US taxpayer and does not intend to become one, then Married Filing Separately is the appropriate tax filing status for you.
- If you don't want to share details of your income with your spouse (or if spouse doesn't want to share details of his / her income with you), then Married Filing Separately may be your filing status of choice.
- It's not only your income that's combined with that of your spouse when you file jointly, your deductions, credits and many other aspects of your return are combined as well. Even when a claim relates to only one of you (for example, a claim for the Foreign Earned Income Exclusion (FEIE), both spouses are effectively associated with it if it is made on a joint return.
- So, if you don't agree with some claim that your spouse intends making in your joint return, or if you suspect that your spouse may not be declaring all his or her income, it's probably better for you to file separately. (There's a procedure called Innocent Spouse Relief, but this is only available where the one spouse didn't know of the issue).
- Married Filing Jointly results in you and your spouse being individually liable for any tax that may be owing. In other words, the IRS can collect the full amount of tax from you, even though the income may have been earned by your spouse. If you don't want to be individually liable for the tax, then Married Filing Separately may be your filing status of choice.

Head of Household

- If you are married, but do not live with your spouse, and pay most of the living expenses of dependents who live with you, it may be best for you to file your return separately from your spouse with Head of Household as your tax filing status.

If You are not Married

Single

- If you are not married, in most cases your tax filing status will be Single. This is the mandatory status if you are not married, unless you happen to support dependents who live with you.

Head of Household

- If you are not married, but support dependents who live with you, it will generally be better for you to choose Head of Household as your tax filing status.

- Head of Household tax rates are lower than Single tax rates for any given level of income.

Qualifying Widow(er)

- If you became widowed in the previous 2 years, have not remarried, and you pay more than 50% of the support for your children who live with you, it will generally be better for you to choose Qualifying Widow(er) as your tax filing status.

- Qualifying Widow(er) status allows you to use the same rates as Married Filing Jointly, which are lower than the rates for Single and Head of Household.

"Married" and "Dependents"

Married

- People entering the US who are regarded as married in their home country are generally regarded as married by the IRS. This includes same sex marriages.

- The actual test is whether the couple would be recognized as married by *any* State in the US (the State need not necessarily be the one where the couple lives).

- The IRS does not recognize a domestic partnership or civil union as a marriage unless it is recognized as a marriage by at least one State in the US.

Dependents

- For the purpose of deciding whether you qualify for Head of Household filing status, a dependent generally includes your parents, children under 19 (or under 24 if studying full time), and permanently disabled children, provided they reside in the United States, live with you, and you pay more than half their support costs.

- Other relatives may also qualify as dependents if they earn little or no income.

Decided Annually

- Although most taxpayers tend to use the same filing status year on year unless their circumstances have changed, your decision on filing status (if your circumstances permit for more than one possibility) can be made annually.

- For example, if you are married, you and your spouse can file separately in year one, and jointly in year two, etc.

- Whether you are regarded as married or unmarried depends on your marital status at the end of the year.

LET'S CELEBRATE! WE'VE BEEN HERE FOR ONE YEAR!
YES! I CAN'T WAIT TO TRY OUT THIS PACKAGE ON OUR FIRST U.S. TAX RETURN!
TAX PREP

Chapter 6

Your First Return

Professionals, Packages and High Street Preparers

The fact that you are reading this book suggests that you are quite unusual as far as US taxpayers go!

This is because very few US taxpayers own foreign (non-US) bank accounts or investments; similarly, very few US taxpayers earn income outside the US; and even fewer are transitioning from non-US taxpayer status, into US taxpayer status. These differences make you very unusual indeed.

This chapter is not intended as a guide for you to prepare your first return. You should not generally prepare your first return, nor subsequent returns, for that matter. Instead, you should select who your return preparer should be.

Packages which otherwise are good, frequently don't deal well with the foreign issues likely to present themselves in preparing your return.

This chapter is intended to act as a guide in selecting your return preparer, and some of the issues likely to arise in relation to your first return.

Your First Return

- Seldom, if ever, do newcomers receive returns from the IRS without asking for them. Notwithstanding the fact that you most likely have not received a return, is up to you to file one, and to file it by the due date, which is generally mid-April of the next year.

- So if you became a US taxpayer at any time during the year, you have to file your return for that year by mid-April of the next year. You can obtain an extension to mid-October by applying to the IRS.

- Once you know or suspect that you have become a US taxpayer, you should contact a return preparer before mid-April of the next year, so they can prepare your return or file for an extension, as the case may be.

- If the preparer you have chosen has the required experience, he or she should be able to take care of all your needs in relation to your return.

Packages, Professionals and High Street Preparers

At the highest level, these are the three broad possibilities that you have for preparing your returns. We'll deal with each of these in a bit more detail below.

Packages (Tax Preparation Software)

- Over the last number of years, software packages have become increasingly popular as a means for people to prepare and file their returns on a DIY basis.

- Much of the appeal lies in the fact that the packages are inexpensive and accessible, and they are easily available both online and in stores; not to mention that they fit right in with the increasing trend of computerization, and the independence that this facilitates.

- In years gone by, some of these packages contained glitches, which caused errors in the return, but by and large, they work fairly well these days, for the users for which they are intended.

- But the users for which these packages are intended does not include you! These packages are designed for the mass market, rather than someone with your foreign interests and the special characteristics that arise when transitioning to US taxpayer status.

- As a result, many of the key issues impacting you are quite unlikely to be recognized by the software, and even if they are, they are unlikely to be properly dealt with. Because of your unusual status and ownership of foreign assets, the software is generally unable to print all the forms you will need to file.

- We sometimes have to bring new entrants into compliance where they have used one of these packages to prepare their returns, and in doing so have unwittingly gone out of compliance.

- The comment above is not intended as a criticism of the packages. On the contrary, they generally do a good job for the average US taxpayer. But you are not the average US taxpayer.

- So however appealing a package may seem, or the package advertisements may be, this is not a good option for you. At least not right now.

High Street Preparers

- Better than using a package, but still not good enough for your circumstances, are walk-in tax return preparation services offered by retail stores.

- Again, these services are aimed at the mass market of US taxpayers. So, while they tend to do a good job for most US individual taxpayers, they are unlikely to do a good job for you.

- Most of these services rely on software to drive the returns (and in some cases, the interview), and the software simply does not recognize your special circumstances, or if it does, it is quite unlikely to be able to deal with them properly, including not being able to print out all the forms you may require to report your non-US investments.

- As a result, they are quite unlikely to be able to prepare a return for you the way it should be prepared. On many occasions we have had to bring new entrants into compliance where they have used one of these services to prepare their returns, and in doing so have unwittingly gone out of compliance.

- This is not intended as a criticism of these services. They generally do a good job for the average US taxpayer. But again, you are simply not an average US taxpayer.

Professionals

- By "professionals" I'm referring to individuals who provide return preparation services, other than in a high street type environment. This potentially includes CPA's, attorneys, and individuals who are neither, but may be an EA (Enrolled Agent) or hold some other form of accreditation.

- Professionals, mostly CPA's, generally do a wonderful job preparing their client's returns. And some attorney firms do a good job too. But you need to be selective.

- The person to prepare your US tax returns should be someone who has had significant recent experience transitioning new entrants into US taxpayer status. Be direct when you ask about this – and be sure to ask what forms the person usually prepares for clients with foreign interests.

- Aside from your actual tax return, which is Form 1040, here's a checklist of some forms the preparer will likely need to prepare. If they don't at least mention most of these forms, you should look somewhere else:

  - Form 8938

    This is to disclose the maximum value of each of your foreign financial assets.

  - Form 5471

    This is to disclose your interests in foreign companies. A separate form generally needs to be completed for each interest. See *Foreign Company Complications*.

o Form 8992

This is to disclose your share of GILTI income if you have interests in foreign companies that are Controlled Foreign Corporations (CFC's). See *Foreign Company Complications*.

o Form 3520

This is to disclose your interest in or transactions with foreign trusts. A separate form generally needs to be completed for each interest. These forms need to be filed separately from your return. See *Foreign Trust Travails*.

o Form 3520-A

This is the tax return for a foreign trust, if it's a Grantor Trust of which you are the owner. A Grantor Trust is a US tax term discussed under *Foreign Trust Travails*. These forms need to be filed separately from your return.

o Form 8621.

This is to disclose your interest in foreign mutual funds. A separate form generally needs to be completed for each interest. See *Mutual Fund Mayhem*.

o Form 1116

This is to quantify your credit for foreign tax that you may have paid.

o Form 2555

This is to claim a Foreign Earned Income Exclusion if you earned active income while living outside the United States.

o Form 114

This is your FBAR. Because FBARs can only be filed electronically these days, you should ensure that your preparer also files your FBAR for you. This form is filed with the US Treasury, not the IRS.

What to Expect

- Your US filings will very likely be more detailed and complex than the returns you filed in your home country.
- Don't be misled by the fact that your US return (Form 1040) has a small number of fields; this is just a summary!
- Unless your circumstances are very simple, your Form 1040 return is more in the nature of a summary of the amounts that are calculated in various other schedules or forms.
- Depending upon your circumstances, in addition to income tax, your return may need to calculate Alternative Minimum Tax (AMT), Net Investment Income Tax (NIIT), Self-Employment (SE) tax, Social Security Tax, Medicare Tax, and Healthcare Tax.

Unless you live in one of the few States that don't levy personal income tax, you will likely also have to file a State tax return. The person who prepares your federal return and schedules should generally also prepare your State return and FBAR.

IRS
IT'S NONE OF THEIR BUSINESS
NON-DISCLOSURE
PENALTIES
DISCLOSURE
FOREIGN ACCOUNTS

Chapter 7

Foreign Bank Accounts and FBARs

You Need to Report Your Foreign Accounts

Whatever the mix of a person's investments may be, I have yet to come across someone moving to the US who does not have at least one foreign bank account.

Because the reporting threshold for foreign bank accounts is fairly low ($10,000 cumulative), virtually everyone moving to the US is required to report their foreign bank accounts.

You will need to report your foreign bank accounts on a Foreign Bank Account Report (FBAR). In most cases you will need to report them as part of your tax return as well.

FBAR reporting has been expanded, so these days you need to FBAR report not only your foreign bank accounts, but most other foreign financial assets as well.

Reporting Your Foreign Accounts

- Once you become a US taxpayer, you need to report your world-wide income on your US returns. See *Your Makeover to a US Taxpayer!*

- You also generally need to report your foreign bank accounts, and most of your foreign financial assets, every year.

- This typically includes foreign bank accounts, shares, stocks, mutual funds, and interests in foreign trusts.

- You do not generally need to report foreign tangible assets, for example, foreign real estate.

  So if you owned non-US real estate - say a house - directly, you are not required to report this (although you would have to report any rental or other income you earned from it).

- However, if instead of owning the same house directly, you owned it via a foreign company in which you held the shares, you would then have to report your holding of the foreign shares.

- In most cases, you have to report the foreign financial asset to the IRS (together with your tax return), and to the Treasury (by way of a Foreign Bank Account Report or FBAR).

Foreign Bank Accounts

It would be impossible to move to the United States without having one or more foreign bank accounts, and most new entrants leave at least some of their foreign bank accounts running.

Bank accounts are the most common foreign financial asset that needs to be reported.

Here are some answers to the questions that frequently arise in relation to foreign bank accounts:

- You need to report all your foreign bank accounts. This includes cheque (current) accounts, deposit accounts, savings accounts, and custodial accounts.

- You need to separately report your different bank accounts. As a practical matter, accounts that have different names or different account numbers (albeit different subaccount numbers), should be separately reported.

- When reporting each bank account, you need to disclose the maximum value of that account during the year. This literally means the maximum value on any day of the year, even if that value only lasted for a short period.

- You should disclose the maximum of each account even where funds have been transferred from one foreign account into another foreign account. Yes, this gives rise to double counting, but you are not being taxed on it.

- Virtually everyone moving to the United States has to report their foreign bank accounts on FBARs. This is because the FBAR reporting threshold is relatively low. The FBAR threshold is reached if your foreign bank accounts, together with your foreign financial assets, have a cumulative value of $10,000 or more. This is dealt with in greater detail below.

- You may also have to report your foreign bank accounts with your tax return on Form 8938.

  If you live in the United States, the reporting threshold is between $50,000 and $150,000, depending upon your filing status and year-end values. If you live outside the United States, the reporting threshold is between $200,000 and $600,000 depending upon whether you were married and year-end values.

- Since the introduction of FATCA, banks in foreign countries that subscribe to FATCA routinely report account details to the IRS. The IRS typically compares these details to those that have been reported by the taxpayers. See *FATCA Is No Fantasy*.

FBARs

- You need to file an FBAR for the year if your foreign bank accounts and other foreign assets had a cumulative value of $10,000 or more during the year.

- Even if your foreign bank accounts and assets did not exceed $10,000, you need to file a FBAR for the year if you had signing power over foreign accounts that had a cumulative value of $10,000 or more during the year.

- Aside from bank accounts, you should generally report on your FBARs any other foreign assets that you own, including securities accounts, commodity futures accounts, option accounts, insurance and annuity policies with a cash value, and mutual fund units.

  If you're in doubt about whether to report a foreign financial asset on your FBAR, it's generally a good idea to report it.

- FBARs are filed with the Treasury. They have nothing to do with your income tax returns, which are filed with the IRS.

- Don't make the mistake of assuming that disclosure of an account on your return exonerates you from filing an FBAR, or vice versa. Separate reporting is required, even though this largely amounts to duplication.

- It's important that the accounts and values that you report to Treasury tie in with those you report to the IRS. They should generally correlate, except for the following:

  - You need to disclose on your FBAR foreign accounts on which you have signing power, but no ownership. There is no similar requirement for your return.

  - You need to report your direct ownership of foreign stocks on your tax return, but you don't need to report these on your FBAR, unless they happen to be PFICs. See *Foreign Company Complications* and *Mutual Fund Mayhem.*

- These days FBARs can only be filed electronically. You should make sure your return preparer prepares and files your FBAR for you.

- Although the FBAR filing date for the year is mid-April of the next year, Treasury currently allows you to file by mid-October.

- Penalties for late or non-filing of FBARs are relatively heavy. The penalty for a "non-willful" failure is generally $10,000, which can be applied to each account for each year. The penalty for a "willful" failure is up to the greater of 50% of the account value or $100,000, and the account holder may be subject to criminal proceedings.

- If for some reason you don't file your FBAR on time, or if the FBAR you filed is inaccurate, you will need professional advice. The late filing of FBARs typically triggers an IRS audit, and if this happens, the IRS will likely hold the view that they have "discovered" you. See *OOPs! We're Out of Compliance!*

SHARE CERTIFICATE
GREAT! WE NOW HOLD MORE THAN 10%!
HOLDING MORE THAN 10% OF A FOREIGN COMPANY HAS CONSEQUENCES!
IRS

Chapter 8

Foreign Company Complications

Complications from holding shares in a foreign company

Most people move to the US not because of the tax rules, but in spite of them. If anything, people find that US tax rules are a detraction from, rather than an attraction to, moving to the United States.

This is particularly apparent for those holding interests in non-US entities when they become US taxpayers.

If you have an interest in one or more foreign companies, foreign mutual funds, or foreign trusts, read on. In some cases, it may actually be better for you to dispose of your interest before you become a US taxpayer. See Getting Your Ducks in a Row.

This chapter deals with owning shares in a foreign company when you become a US taxpayer. The chapters that follow deal with owning units in a foreign mutual fund (see Mutual Fund Mayhem), and owning an interest in a foreign trust (see Foreign Trust Travails).

Classifications Galore – in Summary

- If you own an interest in a foreign company, the starting point is whether the foreign company is seen as a corporation, or whether it is seen as a "pass-through", for US tax purposes.

- It's quite likely that your interest will be seen as an interest in a corporation rather than a pass-through.

- If it's seen as a corporation, the next question is whether the company is seen as a Passive Foreign Investment Company (PFIC – pronounced "peefick").

- If the foreign company is seen as a PFIC, special rules apply. If the company is not seen as a PFIC, your percentage ownership of the company's shares will determine how you will be treated for US tax purposes.

Pass-through vs Corporation

- As mentioned above, for US tax purposes, companies are seen either as "pass-throughs" or as "corporations".

- The overwhelming majority of foreign companies are seen as corporations rather than pass-throughs.

- Only in rare cases are foreign companies seen as pass-throughs for tax.

  This usually happens where the foreign company does not provide limited liability to its shareholders, or where the foreign company has applied to the IRS for pass-through tax treatment.

- So, unless you happen to know or suspect that the foreign company falls into one of these rare categories, you can generally assume that it will be seen as a corporation rather than a pass-through for US tax.

PFIC vs Corporation

If you're still reading this, well done, you've made it through the first classification test!

- Assuming the foreign company is seen as a corporation under the pass-through test mentioned above, the next question is whether the company is seen as a PFIC.
- Foreign mutual funds are invariably PFICs, and as such their PFIC status can easily be predicted. See *Mutual Fund Mayhem*. What follows deals with foreign entities that are not foreign mutual funds.
- Outlined below is a summary of some of the more significant indicators of PFIC status, and the consequences of such status.

The tests for deciding a PFIC
Can make you feel quite seasick
Like a ride on a carousel
Where you really can't tell
If you're on or off with -
The next wait-n-see trick!

Active vs Passive Income

Whether or not the foreign company will be seen as a PFIC depends largely upon whether the company earns active or passive income:

- If more than 75% of the foreign company's income is "passive" (in other words, if most of its income comprises interest, dividends, rents, royalties, or capital gains), it will generally be seen as a PFIC.
- Conversely, if more than 75% of the foreign company's income is "active", then it's unlikely to be seen as a PFIC. Active income is income from the sale of goods and services. But you still have to apply the asset test outlined below.

Active vs Passive Assets

A further test is whether most of the foreign company's assets are "active" or "passive":

- If more than 50% of the foreign company's assets are "passive" (in other words, if most of its assets are loans, shares, intellectual property or other assets that produce passive income), the company will very likely be seen as a PFIC.
- Conversely, if more than 50% of the foreign company's assets are "active" (that is, assets that do not produce passive income), then it's unlikely to be seen as a PFIC (unless it fails the passive income test).

25% Held Entities are Included

In considering the question of active versus passive income and assets, you need to consider the foreign company itself, as well as any other entity in which it holds at least a 25% interest.

- Where the foreign company holds 25% or more of another entity, a pro-rata percentage of the held entity's income and assets are deemed to be that of the foreign company.
- For example, let's assume that the foreign company in which you hold shares earns all of its income from dividends that it receives from a subsidiary; and let's assume that the foreign company has a 75% interest in the subsidiary.
- If the subsidiary earns income only from the sale of goods or services, the foreign company will not be seen as a PFIC. This is because 75% of the subsidiary's income will be imputed to the foreign company, and because the subsidiary's income is active, the foreign company will be seen as earning only active income.
- Conversely, if the subsidiary only earns bank interest, there's a very good chance that the foreign company will be seen as a PFIC. This is because 75% of the subsidiary's income will be imputed to the foreign company, and because the subsidiary's income is passive, the foreign company will be seen as only earning passive income.

- Where the foreign company holds less than 25% of another entity, there is no imputation, so the decision is taken on the income and assets of the foreign company alone.

Okay, so Who's Going Crazy?

Aside from the above tests, other rules occasionally may cause, or may prevent, a foreign company being seen as a PFIC.

I'm guessing what you're likely to be thinking at this point: Give me a break! These rules are difficult to apply, PFIC status is really difficult to determine, and who's going to find out about the US tax status of my foreign company investment anyway?

I sympathize with newcomers making PFIC determinations on their foreign company investments. These determinations can be really tricky.

- So, the practical approach is this – as a first step, you should ask the foreign company whether they have ever been evaluated for US tax purposes, and if they have, whether they are seen as a PFIC.

  In most cases, they will not have been evaluated for US tax purposes, and will not have heard of PFIC status, which is an answer, but not the answer you were hoping to hear.

- Having drawn a blank with the foreign company, it remains either for you, or for a third party, to make the determination.

- Unless it's abundantly clear that the foreign company is not a PFIC on the tests referred to above, you should get professional help to make the determination.

- Conversely, in some cases it will be obvious that the foreign company is a PFIC. For example, where the company holds small percentages of a number of other entities, and earns its income from distributions it receives from these underlying entities.

- Just because a foreign company is not a PFIC in year one, does not mean it is not a PFIC thereafter. Strictly speaking, you or someone on your behalf should make a PFIC determination for each year that you hold shares in the foreign company.

Who's going to find out anyway?

- Most taxpayer returns are not audited by the IRS, and the IRS doesn't generally hunt down taxpayers simply because they suspect their foreign company investments may be PFICs. However, non-disclosure of PFIC status is legally incorrect and too risky.

- You should assume that you will be audited by the IRS (although this may never happen), so if you hold an investment in a foreign company that is a PFIC, this should be disclosed as such.

- If you hold a PFIC, it has to be reported in far greater detail on your tax returns than an investment in a regular corporation, and it also has to be reported on your FBARs. The penalties for failing to report PFICs may include a $10,000 fine for each year a PFIC is not disclosed as such. See *Foreign Bank Accounts & FBARs.*

Foreign Companies that are PFICs

- If the foreign company in which you hold shares is seen as a PFIC:
    - you will be required to make onerous annual PFIC filings for so long as you hold the investment.
    - you will generally be subject to harsh US tax treatment when you receive distributions from the company;
    - you will generally be subject to harsh US tax treatment if you make a gain when disposing of it;

- There are limited exceptions to this treatment, these are mentioned below.

- Foreign mutual funds are invariably PFICs, and as a result are subject to this treatment. See *Mutual Fund Mayhem.*

- For these reasons I recommend to clients that where possible, they should dispose of their investments in PFICs before they become US taxpayers.

- If you happen to hold one or more PFIC interests when you become a US taxpayer, you will need to specifically disclose them. You should generally consider disposing of them as soon as possible.

- For each year that you hold shares in the PFIC:

    - You will be subject to maximum tax rates (generally 40%) on any portion of a distribution that is seen as having been earned from prior year profits;

    - You will be denied long term capital gains tax treatment on any gain you make when you sell your shares.

        - Instead, the gain will be taxed as ordinary income; and any portion of the gain seen as having been earned in prior years will be subject to maximum tax rates (generally 40%);

    - The tax on distributions and gains allocated to prior years will be subject to interest.

        - The interest is calculated as if the tax for each year's allocation has remained unpaid from that year;

    - The above applies to PFIC shares that you hold directly, as well as to PFIC interests that you hold via an interest in another foreign company.

        - So, if you own 50% or more of a foreign company, which owns a PFIC, you are seen as owning a pro-rata percentage of the PFIC.

        - And if you own a share in a PFIC, which owns other PFICs, you are seen as owning pro-rata percentages of the other PFICs.

  - o You may be required to file Form 8621 with your tax return, especially if you received a distribution from the PFIC, or made a gain on selling your PFIC interest.
    - ▪ The IRS estimates that the average time taken to prepare this form is more than 20 hours, and for the related record keeping is more than 16 hours.

- If you hold shares in a PFIC type investment when you become a US taxpayer, you should seek assistance from tax professionals with experience in this area.

Exceptions to Harsh PFIC Treatment

At last – a ray of sunshine! If the foreign entity in which you hold shares is a PFIC, you will not be subject to the harsh treatment described above where:

- The total value of your foreign investments that constitute PFICs is less than $25,000 ($50,000 if you file Married Filing Jointly); or

- The PFIC also constitutes a Controlled Foreign Corporation (CFC).
  - o This is where you own more than 50% of the foreign entity, or where you together with other US taxpayers, own more than 50% of the foreign entity.
  - o However, you will then be subject to CFC reporting, so you may've moved from the fat and into the fire. See below.

Foreign Companies that aren't PFICs

Whew! You're now at the point where you have determined that the foreign company, in which you hold shares, is not seen as a PFIC.

The tax treatment and disclosure of your investment is then driven by the percentage of shares that you hold in the foreign company.

Where you own 10% or less of the foreign company

- If you own less than 10% of the shares and voting rights of the foreign company, then things are fairly simple; in general, you will not have special annual reporting requirements for your investment.

- Of course, any dividends or any other income that you receive from the company is reportable on your return; as is any gain or loss on selling your investment.

- And you will need to disclose the investment as a foreign financial asset when you file your tax return. But you will not have to file detailed disclosures for the company. Consider yourself fortunate.

Where you own more than 10%, but less than 50%, of the foreign company

Here things start ramping up a little:

- You will have to file Form 5471 with the IRS for the year you become a US Taxpayer.

    - This means filing a form that provides an income statement and balance sheet of the company, according to US accounting standards.

- You will also have to file Form 5471 for any year in which your interest in the company changes significantly.

    - From experience, preparing this form can take up to say 10 hours, depending upon the facts, and providing you hold less than 50% of the foreign company.

- The dividends you receive, and the long term gains you may make, will generally be subject to income tax at the favorable rates applicable to long term capital gains, generally 15% or 20%.

- These tax rates depend upon your filing status and if your income exceeds the following thresholds:

	15%	20%
Married Filing Jointly	Above $77,200	Above $479,000
Single	Above $38,600	Above $435,800
Head of Household	Above $51,700	Above $452,400
Married Filing Separately	Above $38,600	Above $239,500

- This favorable treatment assumes that the country in which the company was formed is one with which the US has a Tax Treaty, and that you have held the shares for a minimum period of 60 days, and 90 days for preferred shares.

• As an offset against the income tax mentioned above, you will generally be allowed a credit for foreign income tax you may have paid on the dividend or gain (Foreign Tax Credit). This credit is subject to a number of rules and limitations. See *Your Makeover - To a US Taxpayer!, Foreign Tax Paid.*

• If your income exceeds certain thresholds, the dividends and gains will also be subject to Net Investment Income Tax (NIIT) of 3.8%.

- The thresholds that trigger NIIT are income above $250,000 (Married Filing Jointly), $200,000 (Single and Head of Household), and $125,000 (Married Filing Separately).

- A credit for foreign tax is not allowed against NIIT.

• If your interest, together with the interests of other US shareholders, exceeds 50% of the company, the company is then seen as a Controlled Foreign Corporation (CFC).

- You may be thinking "how do I know who owns the rest of the company, and whether they're US taxpayers?"

- This is a fair question. You can't act on information that you don't know. But in cases where the foreign company is closely held by a small number of individuals, you may well know the answer.

- In deciding whether the 50% threshold has been exceeded, only shareholders who hold more than 10% are taken into account.
- The consequences of the company being seen as a CFC are outlined below.

Where you (and other US taxpayers) own more than 50% of the foreign company.

- Where you own more than 50% of the foreign company, or you together with other US shareholders, own more than 50% of the foreign company, the company is considered a "Controlled Foreign Corporation" (CFC).
- Some of the tax treatment here is similar to that outlined above, in that you need to include in your income the dividends you receive from the company, and any gain you may make on selling your shares in the company.
  - These amounts are generally subject to income tax at the rate of 15% or 20%, subject to your income level and the terms described above;
  - These amounts are generally subject to NIIT of 3.8% (in both cases, depending upon your income levels described above.
- However, in addition you need to include in your personal income your pro-rata share of the company's passive "Subpart F" income. In other words, the company's passive income is "imputed" to you for tax purposes.
  - For example, assuming the company earns interest and dividends of $x, and you are a 60% shareholder, you will generally have to report as income on your US return 60% of $x, even if you did not receive anything from the foreign company.
  - Where the dividends you receive have already been taxed in your hands as an imputation of income, you generally don't pay tax on the receipt of the dividend.

- You also need to include in your personal income your pro-rata share of the company's current year earnings that are regarded as invested in US property.
    - This amounts to another imputation, and is usually based on loans or other investments that the company has made into the United States.
- You further need to include in your personal income your pro-rata share of the company's "GILTI" income.
    - This amounts to yet another imputation, and is essentially based on the company's net income above 10% of the value of its depreciable tangible assets.
- You will generally need to file Form 5471, including an income statement and balance sheet, plus a number of related schedules for the year that you become a US taxpayer, and for each year thereafter.
- You will also need to file Form 8992 if the CFC earned GILTI income for the year in question.
- The preparation time for these Forms can be significant.

GOOD THING THAT MOST OF OUR INVESTMENTS ARE OFFSHORE MUTUAL FUNDS!
YES, SO THERE'S NOTHING FOR THE IRS TO TAX!
FUNDS
UNITS
HOLD IT! COMPLETE ONE PACK OF FORMS FOR EACH FUND, PLEASE!
PFIC
IRS

Chapter 9

Mutual Fund Mayhem

Punishing Treatment for Holding Foreign Mutual Funds

Reactions to the US tax treatment of foreign mutual funds can be very different, depending upon who you are talking with.

New entrants tend to be in disbelief that the tax treatment is so harsh, given that they bought these funds before moving to the US.

The reaction of foreign brokers who sell these funds sometimes borders on hostility, especially if they are closely tied to these funds.

And the funds themselves offer little support, usually responding along the lines of "We've never heard of PFIC status", and "We've never had this problem before".

Unfortunately, foreign mutual funds are usually seen as PFICs for US tax purposes, and as a result the holders are treated harshly when they receive income from the funds. They also have onerous filing obligations. These harsh realities usually come to light when the holders file their tax returns.

Historic Background to Tax Treatment of Foreign Mutual Funds

- For many years US lawmakers have held the perception that some taxpayers use non-US mutual funds as a means of unfairly deferring US tax.
- This is because most mutual funds reinvest profits rather than pay distributions, with the result fund income accumulates without attracting tax, and there are few if any distributions for the IRS to tax.
- As a result, lawmakers introduced Passive Foreign Investment Company (PFIC) legislation, which seeks to counter this perceived abuse, and in doing so, frequently imposes significant hardship on US investors in these funds – including new entrants.

What are Foreign Mutual Funds?

- Foreign mutual funds are non-US entities in which investors' funds are pooled and invested in underlying investments.
- They are open to investment by the public, and provide net asset determinations / the value of their units on a regular basis.

How to Recognize Foreign Mutual Funds by Name

- Depending on the country and specific investment, these funds may be called Mutual Funds, Hedge Funds, ETFs, Unit Trusts or simply Funds.
- Fortunately for identification purposes, foreign mutual funds usually include "Fund" as part of their name. For example, if you hold an interest in a non-US entity that is named, say, "Alpha Growth Plus Fund", there's a good chance that this is a foreign mutual fund.

US Tax Treatment

- For US tax purposes, most if not all these funds constitute PFIC (Passive Foreign Investment Company) investments.

- PFICs are non-US entities whose income comprises dividends / interest from entities other than subsidiaries. As a result, most foreign mutual funds are seen as PFICs.

- Investments in foreign mutual funds are frowned upon by the IRS because fund profits are reinvested rather than paid out as income, so the value of the investment grows without attracting taxable income to the investor. As such, they are perceived as a device that unfairly defers US tax.

- When the holder ultimately receives a payout, either by way of a distribution or by selling the investment, the IRS subjects the income or gain to high US tax rates, and typically imposes penalty interest.

- The combined effect of tax and penalty interest may mean sacrificing most of the distribution or gain in certain cases.

- For a more detailed account of the tax treatment, see *Foreign Companies that are PFICs*, in the previous chapter.

Funds Don't Play Fair

- Unless the fund is brand new, or has no US investors, the chances are the fund knows about the PFIC issue.

- Once a fund knows of the PFIC issue, and has US investors, it should provide their US investors with PFIC reporting packs, to facilitate the investors' reporting to the IRS.

- However, this seldom happens. Very few funds service the PFIC issue by providing PFIC reporting packs.

- To complicate matters, most funds are ignorant (or feign ignorance) about the PFIC issue. As a result, new entrants often experience frustration and concern when making enquiries with foreign funds about PFIC issues.

- This may leave you in a real quandary – not only are you not getting the information that you require, you can't engage with the fund in a meaningful manner.

- It's all very well for a fund to deny the existence and significance of the PFIC issue, but it is you, not they, who is becoming a US taxpayer, and having to file US tax returns and FBARs.
- Unfortunately, the problem does not go away just because the fund refuses to entertain it; in most cases you land up having to deal with it without institutional help.

If You Own Non-US Mutual Funds

- As mentioned above, if you own any non-US mutual fund type investments, the chances are that they are PFICs.
- For this reason, you should dispose of your foreign mutual fund interests before you become a US taxpayer.
- If you are already a US taxpayer and have foreign mutual funds, you can try approaching the fund managers and asking them how they are dealing with the PFIC issue.
- If you are met with assurances that the investment is not a PFIC, this is wonderful news! Ask for a copy of the professional opinion on which this determination is based. You may need it in time to come.
- If they acknowledge that the investment is a PFIC, ask them for a PFIC reporting pack. You will be fortunate to receive one.
- If you do receive a PFIC reporting pack, this should facilitate the disclosures you will be required to make on your return.
  - A PFIC reporting pack should allow you to report the investment on a "Mark to Market" basis.
  - This means reporting as income your pro-rata share of the underlying profits and gains on your US returns each year.
  - In most cases this will relieve a lot of the tax sting that would otherwise attach to this type of investment.
  - Make sure that the person who prepares your return exercises the "Qualified Electing Fund" (QEF) election for the first year that you are a US taxpayer.

- However, as mentioned, in most cases approaching the fund managers on the PFIC issue is unlikely to be productive, so you may well land up having to report your interests without institutional assistance.
- If this happens, make sure to find a tax professional with experience in this area to assist you.

Newcomers often too late do learn
Much is at stake with their tax return!
Foreign shares may a problem be
Unless disclosed for the IRS to see
Yet foreign funds may be even worse
For the unaware they're the real curse!

≈

I THOUGHT WE WERE SMART TRANSFERRING OUR INVESTMENTS INTO A TRUST BEFORE WE LEFT... BUT NOW I'M NOT SO SURE...
AND I THOUGHT RECEIVING MONEY FROM MY FAMILY'S TRUST WOULD BE OKAY... BUT NOW I'M NOT SO SURE EITHER...
FIVE YEAR LOOK-BACK
FOREIGN TRUST PENALTIES

Chapter 10

Foreign Trust Travails

Harsh US tax treatment for your interest in a foreign trust

As mentioned in the previous chapter, new entrants would be well advised to dispose of their foreign mutual fund investments before they become US taxpayers.

Disposing of these investments means that they should sell these interests outright, rather than transfer them, or the proceeds from selling them, to a foreign trust.

This is because any transfer you make to a foreign trust shortly before you become a US taxpayer, will likely be ineffective for US tax purposes.

As a separate matter, if you receive a distribution from a foreign trust after you become a US taxpayer, this may well bring about negative US tax consequences.

US taxpayer contributions to, and distributions from, foreign trusts are usually treated harshly for US tax purposes.

Where practical, you should unwind your interest in foreign trusts before you become a US taxpayer. If unwinding is not practical, you must seek advice.

The IRS perception of foreign trusts

- A while back I met with an IRS Director to discuss new disclosure rules on foreign trusts.

  After exchanging pleasantries, I raised the difficulties that taxpayers would experience trying to comply with the new requirements.

  After a lengthy pause he sighed, looked me in the eye and said: "You know, we're under a lot of pressure from Treasury to deal with foreign trusts".

- He was referring to the perception that foreign trusts have been used as a means of avoiding US tax and disclosure rules, usually by causing the trusts to earn income that would otherwise be earned by the taxpayers themselves.

- This perception has led to a volley of tax rules pitched against foreign trusts.

- The majority of these rules are not aimed at new entrants. However, they are exceptionally broad in application, with the result they apply to new entrants as well as long term US taxpayers.

- This is unfortunate, because the circumstances pertaining to foreign trusts for new entrants tend to be quite different from most other US taxpayers.

Different facts – but same treatment

- Aside from "pre-immigration trusts" (which are dealt with below), where new entrants have a relationship with a foreign trust, in most cases the trust was created long before they became US taxpayers.

- As such, these foreign trusts are frequently an incident of family history, formed by people who were not US taxpayers, with assets and income unrelated to the United States.

- Given that these trusts have nothing to do with the United States, the IRS typically has no interest in these foreign trusts – until a beneficiary, who is a US taxpayer, receives a distribution.

- If you, as a US taxpayer, receive a distribution from one of these trusts, the IRS will have significant interest in the foreign trust and in the distribution.

- So even though the reasons for the foreign trust and the distribution you received may have nothing to do with US tax, you will then be subject to the same harsh rules on foreign trusts that apply to other US taxpayers.

- These rules are objective and inflexible, so the taxpayer's state of mind and objectives are irrelevant.

- As a result, new entrants frequently experience hardship due to these harsh foreign trust tax rules.

Which foreign entities are seen as trusts?

- A threshold question is whether the foreign entity will be seen as a trust for US tax purposes.

- A foreign entity will be seen as a trust if one party (the trustee) holds property for the benefit of another party (the beneficiaries), and the beneficiaries do not use the trust as a business vehicle.

- This somewhat broad and ungainly definition typically covers most family trusts, dynasty trusts, special needs trusts, charitable trusts and foundations – providing the beneficiaries don't use the trust as a vehicle for their business.

- It also potentially covers foreign entities such as a treuhand, bewind, fiducie, and other entities with a variety of local names, if they fall within the terms of the above definition.

Commercial / Business Trusts

- In recent years the use of trusts as a business or commercial vehicle has become popular in some parts of the world.

- In these cases, the trustees hold property for the benefit of the beneficiaries, but the beneficiaries essentially use the trust as a business vehicle, similar to the way that shareholders may commonly use a company for business purposes.

- Although these entities may be set up as trusts, and may constitute trusts for other legal purposes, for US tax purposes they will not generally be seen as trusts. In most cases they will be seen as companies (corporations) or as partnerships for US tax purposes.

- For example, some non-US mutual funds are set up as trusts, and may constitute trusts for general legal purposes. Notwithstanding the fact that they may be trusts, they will generally be seen as companies, and therefore as passive Foreign Investment Companies (PFICs), for US tax purposes.

Foreign Pension / Retirement Funds

- Many countries allow favorable tax treatment to pension funds, retirement funds, provident funds, superannuation or "super" funds, and similar vehicles.

- A number of these funds constitute trusts for US tax purposes.

- A threshold question here is whether the foreign entity satisfies the US tax definition of a retirement fund. In most cases, they don't.

- Those foreign funds that don't qualify as US retirement funds are then seen either as foreign grantor trusts, or foreign non-grantor trusts. This is dealt with in more detail below.

Grantor Trusts

- Assuming the foreign entity is seen as a trust for US tax purposes, the next question is whether it will be seen as a grantor trust or a non-grantor trust.

- The grantor / non-grantor distinction arises purely for US tax purposes; the distinction does not generally exist outside of the US, nor does it generally exist in the US outside of tax.

- Grantor trusts are generally ignored for US tax purposes, at least as far as the Grantor is concerned. The Grantor is typically seen as "owning" the grantor trust, so he is effectively seen as owning the assets of the grantor trust.

- The Grantor is also usually seen as earning the trust's income, and is typically taxed on this income, even though he may not receive it. The purpose of this rule is to prevent grantor trusts being used to avoid tax.

- The fact that the Grantor is taxed on trust income, and the trust is ignored, means that beneficiaries can typically receive trust distributions free of tax, because the underlying income has already been taxed to the Grantor.

- This anti-avoidance rule (taxing trust income to the Grantor) could be turned to advantage, by ensuring that the Grantor was not a US taxpayer.

  Under these circumstances, the Grantor was not taxed on trust income (because he was not a US taxpayer), while the beneficiaries could receive distributions tax-free (because the trust was ignored).

- The IRS regarded this as unacceptable, so the rules were amended to preclude grantor trust status where the Grantor is not a US taxpayer.

- As a result, most foreign trusts these days are not seen as grantor trusts. However, there's a few exceptions, the most significant being "pre-immigration trusts", discussed below.

When US tax rules are discussed
They give meaning to legal fiction
To understand them you really must
Get used to a new form of diction
While many seem strange -
and may cause you to change
Nothing's more strange -
than a foreign grantor trust

≈

Pre-immigration Trusts

- A notable exception to the rule that prevents foreign trusts being seen as grantor trusts exists where the foreign trust is a "pre-immigration trust".
- A pre-immigration trust is a foreign trust that you funded within 5 years of you becoming a US taxpayer.
- So, if you transfer assets to a foreign trust, and then become a US taxpayer within 5 years of the transfer, the trust will be seen as a pre-immigration trust.
- Under these circumstances, you will be deemed to have made the transfer on the day that you become a US taxpayer; and the trust will then be seen as a grantor trust, of which you are the Grantor.
- This rule is designed to prevent a person disposing of his assets to a foreign trust before he becomes a US taxpayer, while retaining the benefit and control of the assets via the trust after he becomes a US taxpayer.
- This rule typically applies where the foreign trust has one or more US beneficiaries. In practice, a foreign trust is considered as having US beneficiaries even if no US beneficiaries exist, unless US beneficiaries are precluded in the trust deed.
- If you are thinking of transferring assets to a foreign trust before you become a US taxpayer, you should obtain advice before doing so.

Tax consequences of a pre-immigration trust

- o You will generally be seen as earning any income that the trust's assets may generate after you become a US taxpayer.
- o As such, you will generally be subject to US tax on this income, even though you may not receive it.

- o You will generally need to file Form 3520 each year after you become a US taxpayer.

  The IRS' estimate of the time required for recordkeeping, learning the law, and preparing Form 3520 is in excess of 50 hours.

- o You will also generally need to file Form 3520-A, which includes an income statement and balance sheet for the trust, each year after you become a US taxpayer.

  The IRS' estimate of the time required for recordkeeping, learning the law, and preparing Form 3520-A is in excess of 40 hours.

Non-Grantor Trusts

- Non-grantor trusts are generally recognized, rather than ignored, for US tax purposes.
- Foreign trusts are typically non-grantor trusts. You can generally assume that a foreign trust is a non-grantor trust unless:
  - o the foreign trust has a US taxpayer as the Grantor; or
  - o you have made a settlement to the foreign trust within 5 years of you becoming a US taxpayer.
- If, after you become a US taxpayer, you receive a distribution from a foreign trust (which will usually be a non-grantor trust):
  - You will generally be taxed on the distribution.

    This is discussed in more detail below.

  - You will generally be liable for penalty interest on that portion of the distribution that is seen as earned by the trust in prior years.

    This is discussed in more detail below.

- You will generally need to file Form 3520 for the year that you receive the distribution.

  As mentioned above, the IRS' estimate of the time required for recordkeeping, learning the law, and preparing Form 3520 is in excess of 50 hours.

  You need to plan for the distribution before it is made. By the time the form is prepared it's too late for planning.

Tax and penalties on foreign non-grantor trust distributions

Example

- Let's assume that a few months after you become a US taxpayer, you receive a distribution from a family trust that was established outside the United States by your parents 15 years ago; and that the trust was funded by your parents, neither of whom are US taxpayers.

- Let's further assume that the assets of the trust comprise equities, from which the trust has earned dividends every year; and as a result, the trust has significant retained income.

  Tax Consequences

  - If you can show that the amount of your distribution is less than the trust's income for the year of the distribution, your US tax on the distribution will be at your marginal US tax rate for the year you receive the distribution.

  - If you receive a distribution that exceeds the trust's income for the year of the distribution, the excess will be seen as paid out of the trust's retained income, and the distribution will be seen as an "accumulation distribution."

    - Because the trust's retained income has built-up over many years, the "throwback rule" will cause you to be taxed as though you received the excess over the period of the build-up.

        - The US tax on this portion will be at the highest individual tax rate for each year. For most past years, the highest individual tax rate was in the region of 40%, so you will generally be taxed at approximately 40% on this portion.

        - Because you are seen as having earned this portion over a number of years, you will be subject to penalty interest for the allocation that is made to each year.

    - If you can show that the trust had no current year income, nor retained income, when it paid your distribution, you will not be taxed on your distribution.

- As appears from the above, the way that you will be taxed largely depends upon the current year income, and prior years' retained income, of the foreign trust; and your ability to demonstrate that the distribution was not funded out of retained income.

- Unless you are able to demonstrate that the distribution was not funded out of retained income, then by default the distribution will be deemed to be paid out of retained income.

- It may be possible to avoid the application of this default rule with careful advance planning.

Foreign Pension and Retirement Funds

- As mentioned earlier, many foreign pension funds, retirement funds, provident funds, superannuation or "super" funds, etc, are seen as trusts, and therefore seen as foreign trusts, for US tax purposes.

- If you have an interest in such a fund, the first question is whether the fund satisfies the US tax code requirements for a retirement fund.

- Unless the fund was designed for US taxpayers, the chances are that it won't satisfy these US tax code requirements, because they are highly specific.

- If the fund was not designed for US taxpayers, the fund will generally be seen as a foreign grantor trust, to the extent of your individual contributions to the fund; and the same fund will generally be seen as a foreign non-grantor trust to the extent that your employer contributed to the fund.

- However, if employer contributions exceeded your individual contributions, the whole fund will likely be seen as a foreign non-grantor trust.

- Depending on the information that is available, dealing with fund payouts as grantor / non-grantor trust distributions may be challenging.

- If you come from a country with which the United States has a Tax Treaty, you should check whether provisions in the Treaty with your home country modify the above.

THERE'S LOTS TO LINE UP!
I WISH THEY'D STAND STILL!
NON-U.S. FUND
U.S. TAPAYER STATUS
NON-U.S. COMPANY
NON-U.S. TRUST

Chapter 11

Getting Your Ducks in a Row!

Positioning yourself to become a US taxpayer

In the months before you become a US taxpayer, you have a once in a lifetime opportunity; namely, to arrange your affairs, such that your assets, and your income profile, are suited to US tax and disclosure requirements.

You really need to be proactive here. This means identifying what needs to be changed, and then taking all the steps required for these changes.

In some cases, this may include delaying the date that you become a US taxpayer.

Whatever you need to do, needs to be done before you become a US taxpayer. In most cases, it's not possible or practical to turn back and "undo" your US taxpayer status after you've become a US taxpayer.

Never again will you have the opportunity to rearrange your affairs without attracting significant US tax consequences. Make sure you use the opportunity wisely and to the fullest extent.

Your US taxpayer status

Determine Date

- You first need to determine approximately when you will become a US taxpayer, as this will reveal how much time you have to position yourself for the change. This will depend upon your individual circumstances. See *The Clock is Ticking!*

- Once you have determined the likely date that you will become a US taxpayer, you should consider whether you have any of the assets, income or interests discussed below.

Take Steps

- If you have any of the assets, income or interests discussed below, you should make a realistic assessment of whether you will be able to take the action that is recommended, before you will become a US taxpayer.

Delay Date

- Where you have doubt about accomplishing what needs to be done before you will become a US taxpayer, you should generally delay the date on which you will become a US taxpayer.

- In most cases, this will mean delaying the date that you enter the United States, and may include delaying the date that your green card is issued, if this is practical.

- In other cases, it may mean departing the United States, and / or making filings to sustain your non-resident status. See *The Clock is Ticking!*

- You will need to consult with an immigration attorney if you intend to delay the issuance of your green card.

Already a US taxpayer?

US Tax Payable

- US tax is generally payable quarterly during the year that you receive the income, and latest by mid-April of the following year.
- Where you live outside the United States, tax can be paid latest by mid-June of the following year, subject to interest.

US Filings

- Forms for any year generally need to be filed by mid-April of the next year where the filer lives in the United States.
- The mid-April filing date can generally be extended to mid-October, provided the extension is filed by mid-April. (The extension applies only to the filing of the forms, not to any tax that may be payable).
- Where the filer lives outside the United States, the forms generally need to be filed by mid-June of the next year.
- The mid-June filing date can generally be extended to mid-October, provided the extension is filed by mid-June.
- Where you need to file for an entity (such as a grantor trust) for any year, the forms generally need to be filed by mid-March of the following year.
- The mid-March filing date can generally be extended to mid-September, provided the extension is filed by mid-March. (The extension applies only to the filing of the forms, not to any tax that may be payable).

If you are out of compliance with your US tax payable or filings, you need to remedy the situation. See *OOPs! We're out of compliance!*

Your assets that have increased in value

Assets that you bought

- If you own bought assets such as stocks, real estate, collector items, or any other items that have increased significantly in value since you bought them, you should consider selling them before you become a US taxpayer. Your decision should be made after taking into consideration foreign country tax consequences.

- If you sell them after you become a US taxpayer, you will typically be subject to US income tax of 15% or 20% of the gain (28% for collectibles), plus 3.8% NIIT (plus State tax, if you already reside in a State by then).

    - Although you will generally get credit for any foreign income tax that you paid on the capital gain, against your US income tax on the capital gain, you will still have a residual US tax liability if the foreign tax you paid was less than 15% or 20% of the gain.

    - Any foreign tax that you paid is not creditable against NIIT, and depending on the State, may not be creditable against State tax.

    - The gain will be calculated as the full difference between cost and selling price. You will not be permitted a "step up in value" for any increase in value that took place before you became a US taxpayer.

Assets that you inherited

- If you own inherited assets that have increased significantly in value since you inherited them, you should consider selling them before you become a US taxpayer. Your decision should be made after taking into consideration foreign country tax consequences.

- If you sell them after you become a US taxpayer, you will typically be subject to US income tax of 15% or 20% of the gain (28% for collectibles), plus 3.8% NIIT (plus State tax, if you already reside in a State by then).

- Although you will generally get credit for any foreign income tax that you paid on the capital gain, against your US income tax on the capital gain, you will still have a residual US tax liability if the foreign tax you paid was less than 15% or 20% of the gain.

- The foreign tax that you paid is not creditable against NIIT, and depending on the State, may not be creditable against State tax.

- The gain will be calculated as the full difference between the market value of the assets on the date you inherited them, and the selling price. You will not be permitted a "step up in value" for any increase in value that took place before you became a US taxpayer.

Assets that you received as a gift

- If you own assets that you received as a gift and they have increased significantly in value since the donor acquired them, you should consider selling them before you become a US taxpayer. Your decision should be made after taking into consideration foreign country tax consequences.

- If you sell them after you become a US taxpayer, you will typically be subject to US income tax of 15% or 20% of the gain (28% for collectibles), plus 3.8% NIIT (plus State tax, if you already reside in a State by then).

    - Although you will generally get credit for any foreign income tax that you paid on the capital gain, against your US income tax on the capital gain, you will still have a residual US tax liability if the foreign tax you paid was less than 15% or 20% of the gain.

    - The foreign tax that you paid is not creditable against NIIT, and depending on the State, may not be creditable against State tax.

    - The gain will be calculated as the full difference between the cost of the assets to the donor, and the selling price. You will not be permitted a "step up in value" for any increase in value that took place before you became a US taxpayer.

If you come from a Treaty country

- If you come from a country with which the US has a Tax Treaty, you should check whether provisions in the Treaty with your home country modify the above.

- If you hold a green card, you should generally not claim Treaty relief.

Payments you expect to receive

- If you expect to receive a significant payment or award, it will generally be better for you to receive the payment before you become a US taxpayer where:

    - Individual tax rates in your home country are lower than in the United States; or where

    - The payment will be tax-advantaged in your home country.

      For example, a number of countries allow payments such as capital gains, retirement fund payouts, and other lumpsum payouts to be tax free or taxed at favorable tax rates.

- In most cases, the receipt of an amount after you become a US taxpayer is taxable in the US, even if it accrued before you became a US taxpayer.

    - For example, if you sell an asset while still tax resident in your home country, and the proceeds are only paid out after you become a US taxpayer, you will generally be taxed in the US on the gain from that sale.

    - A similar principle applies to services – if you earn salary or a fee while still tax resident in your home country, but the payment is only made after you become a US taxpayer, you will generally be taxed in the US on this amount.

- If you come from a country with which the US has a Tax Treaty, you should check whether provisions in the Treaty with your home country modify the above. If you hold a green card, you should generally not claim Treaty relief.

Foreign Shares that you hold

Where the foreign company is a PFIC

- If the foreign company in which you hold shares is a PFIC, you should generally sell the shares, and receive payment for them, before you become a US taxpayer.

- See *Foreign Company Complications, PFIC vs Corporation* to determine whether the foreign company is likely to be seen as a PFIC.

Where you hold more than 50% of a non-PFIC company

- Where you hold more than 50% of a foreign company that is not a PFIC, you should consider reducing your shareholding to 50% or less before you become a US shareholder, especially if the other shareholders are not US taxpayers.

- See *Foreign Company Complications, Foreign Companies that aren't PFICs.*

Where you hold more than 10% of a non-PFIC company

- Where you hold more than 10% of a foreign company that is not a PFIC, you should consider reducing your shareholding to 10% or less before you become a US shareholder.

- See *Foreign Company Complications, Foreign Companies that aren't PFICs.*

Foreign Mutual Funds that you hold

- If you hold units or shares in foreign mutual funds, you should generally sell these interests, and receive payment for them, before you become a US taxpayer.

- See *Mutual Fund Mayhem.*

Foreign Trusts

Existing trusts

- Where you have an interest in a foreign trust that can be unwound, you should do so. Get the assets into your own hands, and terminate the trust, before you become a US taxpayer, unless you are confident that you will not receive any distributions after you become a US taxpayer.

- Unwinding an existing trust may entail counter considerations, and may not be practical, especially where the trust involves other family members who are not US taxpayers. You may also encounter trustee intransigence, transfer costs, and other obstacles to unwinding.

- Where unwinding an existing trust is not practical, it may be necessary to design a solution that averts the usual negative US tax consequences attaching to foreign trusts. There is no "silver bullet" here – the solution needs to be worked at, by taking full consideration of all the facts and interests. See *Foreign Trust Travails, Tax and penalties on foreign non-grantor trust distributions.*

- The required action must be taken before you receive any distributions as a US taxpayer. Once you have received a distribution as a US taxpayer, your options are limited.

Trusts to be formed / funded

- You should not generally transfer assets to a foreign trust if you expect to become a US taxpayer within 5 years of the transfer.

- See *Foreign Trust Travails, Pre-immigration Trusts*

Foreign Share / Option Schemes

- Favorable US tax treatment of share schemes is generally limited to schemes that comply with US tax rules. Most foreign schemes don't comply with US tax rules.

- While most foreign share schemes aren't treated favorably for US tax, in some cases they may bring about not only harsh tax consequences, but penalties as well. For example, employment share option schemes that at the date of the award are regarded as being "in the money" (that is, where the value of the shares at the date of award exceeds the exercise price).

- In light of the above, you should consider disposing of your interest in the scheme (if the scheme allows for this) before you become a US taxpayer.

- If it's not practical to dispose of your interests, you should try have vesting take place before becoming a US taxpayer. Seek professional advice before you do so.

- If it's not practical for vesting to take place before becoming a US taxpayer, you should try have the option award take place before becoming a US taxpayer. Seek professional advice before you do so.

Foreign Retirement and Pension Funds

- If you receive a payout from a foreign retirement fund, foreign pension fund, or similar foreign fund after you become a US taxpayer, this will generally be taxed as ordinary income.

- You should seek payment of your interest in these funds before you become a US taxpayer, especially if payouts are tax advantaged in your home country.

  Where it is not possible for a retirement distribution to be paid before you become a US taxpayer, you should investigate whether you can secure an early payout or withdrawal before you become a US taxpayer.

- If an early payout is allowed, you may need to compare the penalty for taking the payment early (if one applies), with the extra US tax that will be payable if you were to receive the payment after you become a US taxpayer.

- Where an early payout is not possible, you should investigate whether your interest can be commuted into an annuity or similar policy. Before following this option, you should first determine the US tax effect of payouts under the annuity / policy.

I'M SENDING THEIR ACCOUNT DETAILS--NOT BECAUSE I WANT TO BUT BECAUSE I HAVE TO.
FATCA SHMATCA! OUR BANK WOULD NEVER GIVE UP OUR ACCOUNT DETAILS!
THEY'D NEVER GIVE US UP AFTER ALL THE YEARS WE'VE BEEN WITH THEM!
IRS
JUST SEND THE DETAILS!!!

Chapter 12

FATCA is no Fantasy

How your foreign investments get reported to the IRS

When the Foreign Account Tax Compliance Act (FATCA) was first mooted in the US a few years ago, a number of people were incredulous.

The idea that one country (the US), could get financial institutions in other countries to comply with their (US) tax reporting requirements, was seen as far-fetched in the fiscal and financial fraternities.

True, the facility for countries to report taxpayer information to each other had existed for many years under Tax Treaties.

But under Tax Treaties, the IRS has to request the information, in relation to specifically identified individuals (or entities). So, an exchange of information under a Tax Treaty was (and still is) relatively rare.

The difference with FATCA is that account holder information is automatically reported to the IRS by foreign financial institutions.

A large number of financial institutions, situated in many countries, now report information to the IRS about their US account holders, on a routine basis.

FATCA is no fantasy.

Background

- FATCA is a relatively recent US initiative that causes foreign banks and financial institutions to report certain of their account holders to the IRS.
- FATCA is one of many steps taken by the US to enforce compliance with US tax and reporting requirements, outlined below.
- As mentioned in previous chapters, a long-held perception within the US is that certain US taxpayers evade tax through foreign structures and bank accounts.
- In 2007 this caused US legislators to identify a number of countries as "secrecy jurisdictions", and to draft legislation aimed at US taxpayers with accounts in these jurisdictions.
- This legislation was snagged in the legislative process, and so it never became law.
- In a parallel development, the US concluded a number of Tax Information Exchange Agreements (TIEAs) with various jurisdictions.
- This was in addition to the comprehensive Double Tax Agreements (DTAs or Tax Treaties) that the US has with a large number of countries.
- Starting with UBS in 2008, the US instituted criminal proceedings against a number of foreign (mostly Swiss) banks, resulting in banks handing over details of their US account holders in some cases.

FATCA – an overview

- FATCA is the most recent significant US initiative aimed at third party reporting of US taxpayer's foreign financial interests.
- The FATCA legislation was enacted in the US in 2014. A number of countries have since subscribed to cross-border reporting under FATCA.

- Financial institutions in the countries that have subscribed to FATCA include banks and institutions that provide deposit taking, investment services, custodial services, and investment insurance.

- Pursuant to FATCA, the IRS now routinely receives information from foreign financial institutions on their US account holders. This is under a process known as the Automatic Exchange Of Information (AEOI).

FATCA Inside the US

- Within the US, the primary significance of FATCA is that it has increased the disclosure requirements for US taxpayers to report their foreign financial interests.

- This is in addition to the disclosures already required by Treasury under the FBAR rules.

- The disclosures required under FATCA, together with the parallel reporting required under FBAR rules, means that anyone who falls foul of the one, invariably falls foul of the other.

- As a result, failure to report foreign accounts is typically subject to both tax and Treasury penalties. Treasury penalties are harsh.

- In addition, FATCA has created a mechanism for the IRS to receive information on the foreign accounts held by US taxpayers, that simply did not exist in the past.

- From experience, the IRS follows up on at least a good portion of the information they receive under FATCA.

- Where the IRS receives details of a foreign account that the taxpayer has not reported on his tax returns and / or FBARs, the taxpayer will likely be audited by the IRS.

FATCA Outside the US

- Outside the US, FATCA has resulted in a number of countries subscribing to agreements that require financial institutions in those countries to report details of certain account holders to the IRS.

- Foreign financial institutions may have to report these details to their own revenue authority, for onward transmission to the IRS, or may have to report the details directly to the IRS.

- A large number of foreign financial institutions have applied to the IRS, and have been issued FATCA reporting numbers.

- While it's possible that some foreign institutions may be paying lip service to FATCA, it's clear that a number of foreign institutions are actually reporting to the IRS under FATCA.

Automatic Exchange Of Information (AEOI)

- Under the FATCA-inspired Automatic Exchange Of Information (AEOI), a number of foreign financial institutions routinely report to the IRS the non-US financial accounts of individuals who are known to be US taxpayers, or suspected of being US taxpayers, due to any of a number of "indicators".

- If you own a bank or financial account in a country that has subscribed to FATCA, it is reasonably likely that your account will be reported to the IRS once the foreign institution becomes aware of, or suspects, your US status.

Indicators of US Taxpayer Status

The "indicators" that cause a foreign financial institution to report an account to the IRS typically include one or more of the following:

- US passport
- US Social Security Number
- US address
- US telephone number
- Power of Attorney in favor of a US person

Accounts of Entities held by US Taxpayers

- Most FATCA reporting relates to US individual taxpayers who directly own foreign accounts.

- However, FATCA reporting also applies to accounts of foreign entities, that are substantially owned or controlled by US taxpayers, where the primary purpose of the entity is to hold financial assets.

Countries that have signed up to FATCA

Although the list is expanding, the countries that currently have subscribed to FATCA include:

Algeria
Angola
Anguilla
Antigua and Barbuda
Armenia
Australia
Austria
Azerbaijan

Bahamas
Bahrain
Barbados
Belarus
Belgium
Bermuda
Brazil
British Virgin Islands
Bulgaria

Cabo Verde
Cambodia
Canada
Cayman Islands
Chile
China
Colombia
Costa Rica
Croatia
Curaçao
Cyprus
Czech Republic

Denmark
Dominica
Dominican Republic

Estonia

Finland
France

Georgia
Germany
Gibraltar
Greece
Greenland
Grenada
Guernsey
Guyana

Haiti
Holy See
Honduras
Hong Kong
Hungary

Iceland
India
Indonesia
Iraq
Ireland
Isle of Man
Israel
Italy

Jamaica
Jersey
Japan

Kazakhstan
Kuwait
Kosovo

Latvia
Lithuania
Liechtenstein
Luxembourg

Macao
Malta
Mexico
Montenegro
Malaysia
Mauritius
Moldova
Montserrat

Netherlands
Nicaragua
New Zealand
Norway

Panama
Peru
Poland
Paraguay
Philippines
Portugal

Qatar

Romania

San Marino
Serbia
Singapore
Slovenia
South Korea
St. Kitts and Nevis
St. Vincent and the Grenadines
Switzerland
Saudi Arabia
Seychelles
Slovak Republic
South Africa
Spain
St. Lucia
Sweden

Taiwan
Trinidad and Tobago
Turkey
Turks and Caicos Islands
Thailand
Tunisia
Turkmenistan

Ukraine
United Kingdom
United Arab Emirates
Uzbekistan

FATCA vs CRS

- No doubt inspired by the wholesale acceptance of FATCA, countries outside the US have created their analog of cross border reporting, namely Common Reporting Standards (CRS).
- The thrust of CRS is the reporting of accounts and certain transactions by an institution in one jurisdiction, to an authority in another jurisdiction, according to a party's tax residency.

CRS does not apply in the US, and the US is not party to CRS.

S. P. Q. R.
STATEMENTS
PENALTIES
QUESTIONS
RETURNS
YOU ARE OUT OF COMPLIANCE!
BUT WE'RE SUCH GOOD, LAW-ABIDING PEOPLE!
HOW DID WE EVER END UP IN SUCH A MESS?!

Chapter 13

OOPs! We're Out of Compliance!

Falling Out of Compliance - and what to do about it

New entrants frequently fall out of compliance with their US tax and Treasury filing requirements.

This is hardly surprising, given the large number and specificity of these filing requirements - especially for holders of foreign financial assets.

And sometimes people become US taxpayers without being aware of it, which inevitably leads to compliance issues.

While there are a number of reasons for falling out of compliance, most who land in this position go through a range of emotions, which typically include disbelief and mild panic.

Yet in virtually all cases, the problem can be solved through appropriate remedial action.

What's important is that you act promptly, and take the correct remedial action.

US Taxpayer Status

- It may come as no surprise that the question whether a person is in, or out of, compliance frequently hinges on whether he or she was a US taxpayer at the relevant time.
- This is because US tax and disclosure requirements are irrelevant unless and until you become a US taxpayer (although income earned in the United States is always subject to US rules).
- But once you become a US taxpayer, you immediately become subject to a significant number of tax and reporting requirements. Especially if you have foreign financial assets. See *Your First Return, Professionals*.

Falling Out of Compliance - Some Common Examples

- New entrants fall out of compliance generally because they haven't filed the required forms, or haven't filed them accurately.
- For example, you will be out of compliance if you have become a US taxpayer and you:
    - Didn't file Form 1040 each year;
    - Filed Form 1040 each year, but didn't disclose all your foreign income;
    - Filed Form 1040 each year, but didn't disclose all your foreign financial assets on Form 8938;
    - Filed Form 1040NR;
    - Didn't file Form 114 (an FBAR) each year;
    - Filed an FBAR each year, but didn't disclose all your foreign bank accounts and financial assets;
    - Have an interest in a foreign company, but didn't file Form 5471;
    - Have GILTI income from a foreign company, but didn't file Form 8992;

  - o Have an interest in a foreign mutual fund, but didn't file Form 8621 each year;
  - o Had a transaction with, or interest in, a foreign trust, but didn't file Form 3520;
  - o Are considered the owner of a foreign grantor trust, but didn't file Form 3520-A;
  - o Received a foreign gift or inheritance, but didn't file Form 3520.

- In most cases, you should have filed the relevant Forms by mid-April of the following year. If you live outside the United States, you can generally file by mid-June of the following year. See *Getting Your Ducks in a Row.*

- So if you became a taxpayer during 2018, you generally should have filed the relevant 2018 Forms by mid-April (or mid-June) 2019, and will need to file the 2019 Forms by mid-April (or mid-June) 2020, etc.

  These dates can generally be extended, provided you apply for extension before the relevant due date. See *Getting Your Ducks in a Row, Already a US Taxpayer?, US Filings.*

Filing Forms after the Due Date

- Assuming there's no tax owing, the average US taxpayer can generally file his tax return after due date without attracting a penalty, and without triggering a tax audit.

- However, new entrants typically have significant reporting requirements in addition to their tax returns, because they have to report their foreign assets and foreign entity interests.

  - o The penalty for late filing these forms is generally $10,000 per form per year.
  - o If you were to simply to file these forms after due date this would typically attract heavy penalties.

- o Furthermore, if you were simply to file FBARs after due date, this would likely trigger an IRS audit.

- In view of the above, if you have fallen out of compliance, you generally should not simply file the forms late. Instead, you should come into compliance under a remediation program, outlined in more detail below.

Remediation Programs

- If you are out of compliance, it will generally be best for you to come into compliance under a remediation program for non-compliant taxpayers, especially if you have both tax and FBAR compliance issues.

- There are two main types of program, one of which provides protection from criminal prosecution, but not from civil penalties; and the other provides protection from civil penalties, but not from criminal prosecution.

  So a threshold issue is whether you have *real* exposure to criminal prosecution.

- Most newcomers who are out of compliance don't have real exposure to criminal prosecution.

  However, because of the fundamental consequences, it's critical to deal with this question as a threshold issue, and for a responsible determination to be made. Make sure that the person who makes the determination has experience in this area.

- Once the question of criminal exposure has been resolved, and the correct program has been determined, it's essential that all the requirements of that program are followed comprehensively and accurately.

  Where the facts Indicate real risk of criminal prosecution

  - o In most if not all of these cases, the individual should come into compliance under Voluntary Disclosure.

  - o Here the focus is on avoiding prosecution. While an absolute guarantee against prosecution is not generally available (because the decision whether to prosecute lies with the Department of Justice, not the IRS), in most Voluntary Disclosure cases, the IRS does not seek prosecution.

- In cases of this nature, it can be expected that significant civil penalties will apply. Depending upon the circumstances, the penalties can be the greater of $100,000 or 50% of undisclosed account balances.

- The OVDI (Offshore Voluntary Disclosure Initiative) and OVDP (Offshore Voluntary Disclosure Program) no longer operate. So, anything you may have read about these programs is unlikely to be relevant.

Where the facts indicate no or low risk of criminal prosecution

- In most of these cases, you should come into compliance under the Streamlined Filing Program.

- Here there is no protection against prosecution, and the focus instead is on minimizing penalties.

- Applicants are required to certify that they were non-willful in falling out of compliance, and they also have to provide a detailed explanation of how and why they fell out of compliance.

- The IRS generally reviews these factors in deciding whether the applicant was non-willful.

- Based on the facts, sound judgement needs to be exercised in deciding whether an individual is a good candidate for the Streamlined Program.

- Under the Streamlined Program, the sought-after objective is a zero civil penalty, which is only possible if you have been living outside the United States.

- If you have been living in the United States, the sought-after objective under the Streamlined Program is a civil penalty of 5% of the foreign undisclosed accounts.

- In a small number of instances, it may not be necessary to apply under the Streamlined Program. These are few and far between, due to the heavy penalties that normally apply for being out of compliance with foreign asset reporting. Sound judgement needs to be exercised in deciding not to apply under this Program.

You, rather than the IRS, should identify and report the problem

- Once you discover, or even suspect, that you are out of compliance, you should waste no time in seeking professional help to identify whether a problem really exists.

- Unless the issue is totally minor, it's quite likely that you will need to make filings, and possibly amended filings, under an IRS remediation program.

- It's far better for you (with professional assistance) to identify the problem and take remedial action, rather than for the IRS to do so.

- Penalties and the IRS treatment tend to be a lot milder when you come forward with compliance issues, rather than when the IRS "discovers" them.

WELCOME TO THE
UNITED STATES OF ACRONYMS
THEY SURE HAVE A LOT OF THEIR OWN TERMS!
NOT TO MENTION A BUNCH OF ACRONYMS!

Chapter 14

United States of Acronyms

Some US Tax Terms and Acronyms

Many years ago, before I moved to the United States, I was employed by a large US-based CPA firm.

At first, I found myself irritated with the acronym-laden language that my US colleagues constantly used when they discussed tax matters.

But then I realized that they had good reason for talking in this fashion; not using acronyms would have exhausted them, and any listeners would have fallen asleep.

There are a large number of US tax terms and acronyms, some of which are used freely with the expectation that the listener will recognize them and understand what they mean.

Listed in the pages that follow you will find the common terms and acronyms, and some other references that will help in your encounters with tax and disclosure.

Accuracy Penalty	A penalty of 20% of the tax underpaid that is generally imposed when income on a tax return is understated.
Accumulation Distribution	This is a distribution from a foreign Non-Grantor Trust that has accumulated income. It's usually taxed heavily with penalty interest.
AEOI	**Automatic Exchange Of Information.** Under FATCA, subscribing foreign financial institutions automatically report to the IRS bank and financial accounts owned by US taxpayers.
AFR	**Annual Federal Rate**. This is the official interest rate that the Federal Reserve publishes on a frequent basis. It is also the interest rate charged if you pay tax late.
AGI	**Adjusted Gross Income**. Essentially, this is the figure comprising your worldwide income.
AMT	**Alternative Minimum Tax**. Tax rules that ensure individuals pay tax above certain threshold amounts.
Basis	US tax term for tax value. Generally, it's the cost of an asset.
Boot	Nothing to do with footwear or your car. This is the US term for the part of a claim that is not allowed.
Cash Basis	Most US taxpayers are taxed on a cash basis. This means being taxed on cash received. This is the default status for individuals.
CFC	**Controlled Foreign Corporation**. Generally, a foreign company that is mostly owned by US Taxpayers.

CTB	**Check the Box**. A set of rules that allows certain companies and other entities either to be regarded as transparent or to be recognized as taxpayers for US purposes.
C Corp	**C Corporation.** Generally, an entity formed in the US that is recognized as a corporation for tax purposes.
CFR	**Code of Federal Regulations.** This includes the Treasury Regulations that apply to tax.
CI	**Criminal Investigation.** The branch of the IRS that undertakes criminal investigations. They also approve applicants under remediation programs.
Code	In the context of tax, this refers to the Internal Revenue Code. See IRC.
Corp	**Corporation**. For US tax purposes, generally a company or corporation that is taxable as an entity.
Corpus	Nothing to do with a dead body. This is a tax term for the capital that has been contributed to a trust.
Deductions	Individuals can claim certain non-business deductions, and business deductions, against their income for tax purposes.
Delinquent Return	A return that should have been filed.
DIF	**Discriminant Inventory Function**. A program the IRS uses to attribute a score to taxpayers depending upon their circumstances. Taxpayers with a higher DIF score are more likely to undergo an IRS audit.

Disregarded Entity	An entity that the IRS disregards for tax purposes. Generally, it's a company with a single shareholder that does not elect to be taxed as a corporation.
DTA	**Double Tax Agreement.** The US has comprehensive DTA's with about 70 countries. See Tax Treaty.
Dual Resident	Your status if you were tax resident in your home country under their domestic rules, while also being tax resident in the United States under US domestic rules.
Dual Status	Your tax status if, during the same year, you were both a US taxpayer for portion of the year, and also a non-US taxpayer for portion of the year.
EIN	**Employer Identification Number**. A number that the IRS issues to an entity, irrespective of whether it employs anyone.
Election	Nothing to do with politics. Any of a number of tax-related choices that are available to US Taxpayers.
Estimated Tax	Tax that generally needs to be paid every quarter if you earn income that is not subject to US withholding tax.
ESOP	**Employee Share Option Trust.** Nothing to do with fables, it's an acronym for Employee Stock Ownership Plans. Most foreign plans don't qualify.
Examination	Nothing to do with going to the doctor. This is an IRS audit.
Exemption	An amount of income that is not subject to US tax.

FATCA — **Foreign Account Tax Compliance Act.** An acronym for rules that cause foreign banks to report accounts owned by US taxpayers.

FBAR — **Foreign Bank Account Report.** A Treasury form that you need to file annually to report your non-US bank and financial accounts. See Form 114.

FDAP — **Fixed, Determinable, Annual, Periodical.** The acronym for passive income that is typically subject to a 30% withholding tax when earned by nonresidents, unless reduced under a Treaty.

FEIE — **Foreign Earned Income Exclusion.** Non-US salary and housing benefits, that may be exempt from US tax. The current limit is slightly over $120,000.

FEIN — **Federal Employers Identification Number.** See EIN.

FICA — **Federal Insurance Contribution Act.** Generally, this refers to Social Security Tax and Medicare Tax, which together comes to 15.3% of salary, wages, and self-employment income.

Figure — American for calculate. It has nothing to do with body shape.

File — This generally means mailing or electronically submitting your return.

Filing Status — This is your tax filing status after you become a US Taxpayer. It depends upon your lot in life. It is either Single, Married Filing Jointly, Married Filing Separately, or Head of Household.

Filing Threshold	If you earn above this amount, you have to file a US return for the year.
FIRPTA	**Foreign Investment in Real Property Tax Act**. Far-reaching rules for taxing nonresidents on their gains from US real estate.
FTC	**Foreign Tax Credit**. This is a credit against your US tax for the foreign tax you have paid on your foreign income.
Form 114	This is a Foreign Bank Account Report (FBAR).
Form 1040	The US income tax return that you generally have to file annually once you become a US Taxpayer. Not to be confused with Form 1040-NR, which is a Nonresident return.
Form 1040-NR	The US income tax return you may need to file if you earn US income before you become a US taxpayer.
Form 1042	A form that US banks, brokers or other payors will send you if you have earned income from or through them, and you are not a US taxpayer. They also send a copy to the IRS.
Form 1099	A form that US banks, brokers, and other payors will send you if you have earned income from or through them. They also send a copy to the IRS.
Form 1116	The form you need to file to calculate and claim credit for the foreign tax you have paid.
Form 3520	The form you need to file to disclose transactions with a foreign trust; of if you are the Grantor of a foreign grantor trust; or if you derive a foreign gift or inheritance.

Form 3520-A	Another form you need to file to disclose annually if you are the Grantor of a foreign grantor trust.
Form 5471	The form you frequently need to file if you hold shares in, or are an officer of, a foreign company.
Form 8621	The form you need to file if you hold an interest in a foreign mutual fund such as an ETF or unit trust.
Form 8938	Another form you generally need to file if you hold foreign accounts or assets.
Form 8992	The form you need to file if you have an interest in a CFC that has earned GILTI income.
Form W-2	The form you will receive from your US employer. They also send a copy to the IRS.
FPHC	**Foreign Personal Holding Company.** If you have one, this is a holding company for your foreign investments. These days its main relevance is that it's likely a PFIC.
Fraud Penalty	A penalty of 75% of the tax underpaid that is attributable to fraud.
GAAP	**Generally Accepted Accounting Principles.** The US standards for accounting, compared to IFRS (International Financial Reporting Standards) or other country standards.
GILTI	**Global Intangible Low Taxed Income.** Income that is imputed to a US taxpayer, if he is a shareholder in a foreign company which: is a CFC, earns income from intangibles, and is subject to low rates of foreign tax.

Grantor	A person who has funded a trust
Grantor Trust	A trust that is effectively ignored for US tax purposes, with the result that trust income is generally taxed to the Grantor(s).
Green Card	A card issued by the USCIS (previously, the INS) evidencing the holder's right to permanent residence in the United States.
HOH	**Head of Household**. A tax filing status, available where spouses do not live together, have dependents, and one spouse has borne most of the expenses of the household.
Information Return	A form that is required to be filed with the IRS other than a tax return.
Inventory	A term that is frequently used in the US for stock (of goods).
IDR	**Information Document Request.** This is the type of letter you will receive if you happen to undergo an IRS examination.
IRA	**Individual Retirement Account.** These generally qualify for favorable US tax treatment. Foreign retirement accounts generally don't.
IRC	**Internal Revenue Code.** This is the source of the rules that govern your taxes. Together with the Regulations, these rules run to about 80,000 pages.
IRS	**Internal Revenue Service.** The US government agency tasked with tax administration. They also administer FBARs on behalf of Treasury.

IRSN	**Internal Revenue Service Number.** An identifying number that the IRS may issue if you don't have a social security number nor an ITIN, or these are unknown.
ISO	**Incentive Stock Option.** These plans are generally tax advantaged in the US. Most foreign plans do not qualify for these advantages.
Itemized Deductions	Specific deductions that you can claim on your tax return instead of claiming a standard deduction.
ITIN	**Individual Tax Identification Number.** A tax number issued by the IRS to individuals who need to file US returns but do not have a social security number.
K-1	**Schedule K-1.** A form that a partnership, S Corp, trust or estate will likely issue to you showing the income that you earned. They will send a copy of the form to the IRS.
LB&I	**Large Business & International.** The section of the IRS that deals with most cross-border issues. They also support regular agents.
LLC	**Limited Liability Company.** Typically, this is a company formed in one of the States. It may or may not be a separate taxpayer.
LOB	**Limitation On Benefits.** An article of most US tax treaties that limits the ability to use the treaty unless you are resident in the treaty country.

LTCG	**Long Term Capital Gain.** A capital gain that is subject to a favorable rate of tax where you have held the asset for more than 1 year. The acronym is used occasionally.
MFJ	**Married Filing Jointly**. The tax filing status that most married couples choose due to the rate and other advantages over Married Filing Separately.
MFS	**Married Filing Separately**. The tax filing status that married couples occasionally choose due to specific tax or personal reasons.
Medicare Tax	A tax of 2.9% on US salary, wages and self-employment income. Half of the tax is paid by the employer, and the other half by the employee. Additional Medicare Tax of 0.9% is payable on similar income above certain thresholds.
Miscellaneous Penalty	Generally this refers to a penalty for failing to comply with tax and FBAR under a remediation program.
NIIT	**Net Investment Income Tax.** A tax of 3.8% on investment income earned above certain thresholds.
NOL	**Net Operating Loss.** A tax loss which you can carry over to other tax years, subject to certain rules.
Non-Grantor Trust	A trust that is not a grantor trust. Non-grantor trusts are generally recognized as taxable entities for US tax purposes.
Non-willful Penalty	The penalty imposed for failing to file, or to make the required disclosures, on FBARs, if you can show this was unintentional.

OVDI / OVDP	**Offshore Voluntary Disclosure Initiative / Program.** A specific voluntary disclosure program that no longer operates.
Pass-thru	This is used to describe certain companies and other entities that are not recognized as taxable entities for US tax purposes.
Phase-out	This is used to describe the limitation of deductions or exemptions above certain income levels.
PFIC	**Passive Foreign Investment Company.** A foreign entity that mostly earns passive income. Gains and distributions received from PFICs are taxed harshly.
Pre-immigration Trust	A foreign trust to which assets were transferred within 5 years of the transferor becoming a US taxpayer.
Qualified Dividends	Dividends you may receive that qualify for Long Term Capital Gains tax rates.
Reasonable Cause	What taxpayers need to illustrate if they wish to reduce or avoid certain penalties.
REIT	**Real Estate Investment Trust.** A US entity that owns US real estate and qualifies for favorable tax treatment.
Retirement Plan	A plan such as an IRA or 401(k) plan which is tax advantaged for US tax. Most foreign retirement plans do not qualify.

Schedules	There are 5 schedules that commonly need to be included with your tax return Form 1040: **Schedule A** – Itemized Deductions. To be completed if you want to claim specific deductions, rather than a Standard Deduction. **Schedule B** – To be completed if you earn interest or dividends exceeding $1,500, or have foreign account / trust interests. **Schedule C** – Sole Proprietor. To be completed if you operate a business or practice as a sole proprietor. **Schedule D** – Capital Gains and Losses. To be completed if you disposed of any capital assets. **Schedule E** – Rental and Entity Income. To be completed if you earned rental income, or if you earned income from a US partnership, S corporation, trust or estate.
S Corp	**S Corporation.** Generally, an entity formed in the US that is a pass though for tax purposes.
SE Tax	**Self Employment Tax** – A tax of 15.3% required to be withheld on self-employment income. It comprises social security tax of 12.4%, and Medicare tax of 2.9%.

Social Security Tax — A tax of 12.4% on salary and wages. Half of the tax is paid by the employer, and the other half is paid by the employee.

If you are not a US taxpayer, you may still be liable for this depending upon your visa type and the terms of a Totalization Agreement (if one exists).

SSN — **Social Security Number**. A number issued to qualifying individuals by the Social Security Administration. Once issued, it is used as the individual's tax number.

Standard Deduction — The deduction that is allowed on your tax return if you don't claim itemized deductions.

Statute — **Statute of Limitations.** This generally refers to period of prescription within which the IRS may institute proceedings.

Stock — The term frequently used in the US for shares in a company.

Streamlined Program — A remediation program for taxpayers who are out of compliance. It can be beneficial or problematic, depending on taxpayer circumstances.

Subpart F Income — Income that is imputed to a US taxpayer, if he is a shareholder in a foreign company which earns passive income and is a CFC.

Tax Resident — This is sometimes used to describe an individual who is a US taxpayer.

Tax Year — The tax year is generally the calendar year for US tax purposes.

Tax Treaty

This generally refers to a Double Tax Agreement, which is a comprehensive income tax treaty between the US and another country. There are about 70 of these.

There are also Tax Information Exchange Agreements, Estate Tax Treaties, and Totalization Agreements.

Throwback Rule

Rules that cause distributions from foreign non-grantor trusts to be "thrown back" and seen as distributed in previous years.

TIEA

Tax Information Exchange Agreement. An agreement between the US and one of a number of countries to exchange information. These fall short of comprehensive tax treaties.

TIN

Tax Identification Number. For most US taxpayers, this is their social security number. If you do not have, nor qualify for, a social security number, it should be your Individual Tax Identity Number (ITIN).

Totalization Agreement

An agreement between the US and one of about 25 foreign countries to regulate social security arrangements.

USRPHI

United States Real Property Holding Interest. Generally, the interest that non-US taxpayers hold in a US entity that holds US real estate. This is relevant for FIRPTA.

W-2

The form you will generally receive from a US employer with details of your salary and deductions. A copy is sent to the IRS.

W-4

A form you will need to complete if you take employment in the US to determine your exemptions from withholding tax.

W-7

An application for an Individual Tax Identification Number. Generally original or notarized copies of supporting documentation need to accompany the application. See ITIN.

W-8BEN

A form that non-US taxpayers usually provide to US payors of income that they will earn. It's essentially a notification of foreign status.

W-9

A form you may need to provide to a US payor of income that provides details of your US taxpayer status.

Tax Treaties

Commentary on tax treaties has been included by way of appendix. This is because claims based on tax treaties aren't frequently made for a variety of reasons, some of which are more valid than others.

Using a treaty to support your claim that you're not a US taxpayer

- Most new entrants to the US hold a green card, or will shortly acquire one. They should not make use of a tax treaty with their home country to secure relief from US tax for any period after they have been issued a green card, because doing so will jeopardize their green card.

- However, there are cases where new entrants may be able to benefit from a tax treaty without jeopardizing their green card. This typically arises where the new entrant has not yet been issued a green card, and is not about to acquire one; and

    - Was admitted into the US under a visa waiver program; or

    - Was admitted into the US under a visa category such as B, H, K, or L, that does not suspend the running of the time-related formula.

      This is because visa categories F, J, M and Q generally suspend the running of the time-related formula, with the result there's generally no need to rely upon a treaty to avoid becoming a US taxpayer (see *The Clock is Ticking!, Time-Related Formula)*; or

    - Was admitted into the US under visa category F, J, M or Q, and the new entrant has fallen out of compliance with this visa, with the result the visa has become invalid or has lapsed.

- If you are one of the new entrants described above, depending upon your circumstances, you may be able to argue that the treaty with your home country has shielded you from becoming a US taxpayer.

- For this to arise, you would typically need to be regarded as tax resident in your home country (under your home country's tax rules), and would also need to be regarded as tax resident in the US (under US rules - typically because you have spent more than 183 days in the US under the Time-Related Formula test. See *The Clock is Ticking!*).

- If the above applies to you, you may be able to use the "tie breaker" provisions of the treaty to support a claim that you should not be regarded as a US taxpayer.

- Tie breaker provisions are designed to attribute tax residence to only one of the two treaty countries. These provisions only apply when the respective domestic tax rules of each country determine that you are tax resident in that country.

- For you to succeed under the tie breaker rule in most treaties, the following will generally need to apply:

    - You will need to have a permanent home available to you in your home country, but not in the US; or

    - If you have a permanent home available to you in both countries, then you need to have closer personal and economic relations in your home country, than in the US; or

    - If it cannot be determined in which country you have closer personal and economic relations, then you need to have an habitual abode in your home country, but not in the US; or

    - If you have an habitual abode in both countries, or in neither of them, then you need to be a citizen of your home country.

    (Because the tests outlined above vary slightly in some treaties, the wording in the treaty with your home country will need to be checked before the tests are undertaken).

- If the above applies to your circumstances, you may claim that you are not a US taxpayer. Make sure that the tax professional preparing your claim has experience in this area.

If under the tiebreaker test you're tax resident in the US rather than in a foreign country

- The most common way that treaties reduce US tax for new entrants is by "overriding" your US taxpayer status under the tie breaker test on the basis outlined above, thereby having you regarded instead as a non-US taxpayer.

- If your factual circumstances don't qualify you for an override of your US taxpayer status under the tie breaker test, you generally can't use a treaty to reduce your US tax on an item of income - even though the income may fall within one of the treaty reduction provisions.

- This is because most US treaties contain a "savings" provision, which allows the US to tax US taxpayers as though the treaty does not exist. However, sometimes treaty reduction provisions relating to pensions and occasionally other types of income are excluded from operation of the savings provision – with the result these benefits can be claimed by US taxpayers. Because the wording of the savings provision varies between treaties, the wording in the treaty with your home country will need to be checked before you follow this route.

After you become a US taxpayer - Using a US treaty to reduce your foreign income tax

- Once you have become a US taxpayer, you may be able to use a US tax treaty with your home country to reduce the foreign country tax on your income.

- There's a common misperception that the US foreign tax credit (whereby US taxpayers get credit against US tax for the foreign tax they have paid) removes the incentive to reduce foreign tax.

- This perception is based on a misunderstanding of the US foreign tax credit rules, because a foreign tax credit is limited to taxes paid in a foreign country that cannot be reduced or refunded.

- So to the extent the foreign tax you pay is susceptible to reduction or elimination under a treaty, a US foreign tax credit is not available; under these circumstances, instead of claiming a foreign tax credit in the US, you should instead apply (in the foreign country) for relief under the treaty.

List of Treaties

Set out below is a list of the countries with which the US has a comprehensive income tax treaty (Double Tax Agreement or DTA). These are not to be confused with other types of tax treaty, for example Tax Information Exchange Agreements (TIEAs), or Estate Tax Treaties.

Armenia
Australia
Austria
Azerbaijan

Bangladesh
Barbados
Belarus
Belgium
Bulgaria

Canada
China
Cyprus
Czech Republic

Denmark

Egypt
Estonia

Finland
France

Georgia
Germany
Greece

Hungary

Iceland
India
Indonesia
Ireland
Israel
Italy

Jamaica
Japan

Kazakhstan
Korea
Kyrgyzstan

Latvia
Lithuania
Luxembourg

Malta
Mexico
Moldova
Morocco
Netherlands
New Zealand
Norway

Pakistan
Philippines
Poland
Portugal
Romania
Russia

Slovak Republic
Slovenia
South Africa
Spain
Sri Lanka
Sweden
Switzerland
Tajikistan
Thailand
Trinidad
Tunisia
Turkey
Turkmenistan

Ukraine
Union of Soviet Socialist Republics (USSR)
United Kingdom
Uzbekistan
Venezuela

Made in the USA
Monee, IL
11 November 2026

68342110R00095